Table of Contents

Maps:

Map Trek: Atlas of the World & U.S. History – pages 6, 40, and 52.

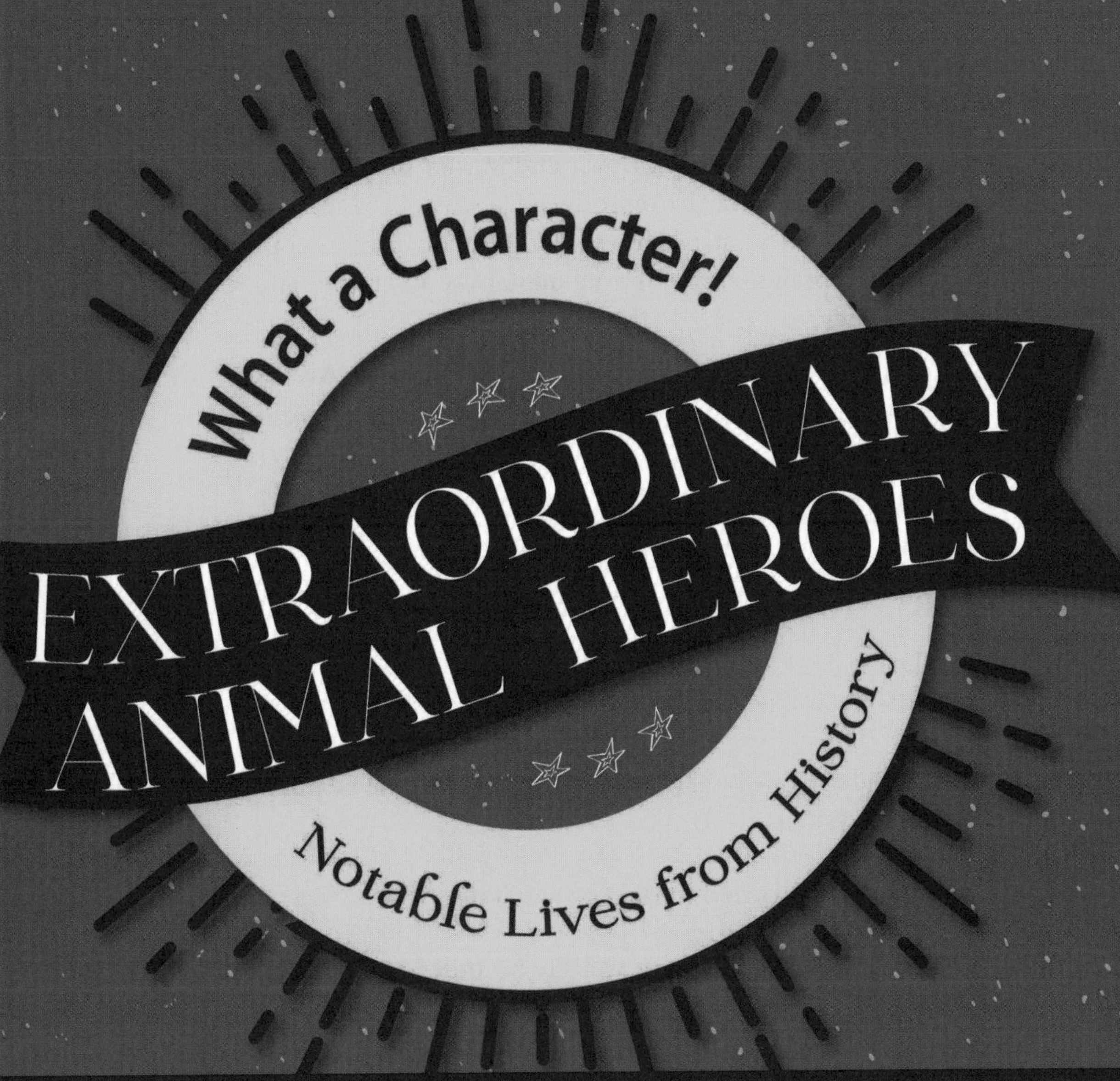

Marilyn Boyer

First printing: March 2024

Master Books, P.O. Box 726, Green Forest, AR 72638

Master Books® is a division of the New Leaf Publishing Group, LLC.

ISBN: 978-1-68344-362-9
ISBN: 978-1-61458-877-1 (digital)
Library of Congress Control Number: 2024931280

Cover: Diana Bogardus
Interior: Terry White

Please consider requesting that a copy of this volume be purchased by your local library system.

Printed in the United States of America

Please visit our website for other great titles:
www.masterbooks.com

For information regarding promotional opportunities, please contact the publicity department at pr@nlpg.com.

World War I

World War I, often called the Great War, was fought from 1914–1918. Franz Ferdinand, **archduke** of Austria-Hungary was **assassinated** along with his wife, Sophie. The killer was a Serbian man who believed parts of Austria actually belonged to Serbia. Austria-Hungary, blaming the Serbian government, declared war on Serbia one month later. Europe at the time of the conflict was divided into two major powers — Germany and Austria-Hungary. Later, the **Ottoman Empire** joined the Central Powers. The Allied Powers were Great Britain, France,

archduke: Son of the Emperor of Austria

assassinated: Murdered

Ottoman Empire: An empire developed by Turks between the 14th and 20th centuries

and Russia. Later, they were joined by Italy. The United States at first remained **neutral**. In May 1915, the passenger ship RMS (British Royal Mail Ship) *Lusitania* was sunk by a German submarine, killing 128 Americans. This, of course, greatly upset the Americans. In February 1917, the United States learned that Germany had secretly tried **enticing** Mexico to attack the U.S. On April 6, the U.S. government, headed by President Woodrow Wilson, officially declared war on Germany, and by December 1917, 175,000 U.S. troops were in Europe. With the added strength of the United States, the Allies would win the war in November 1918, but before then it would be a difficult fight for the Allies.

neutral: Not helpful or supportive of either side in a conflict

enticing: Attempting to persuade

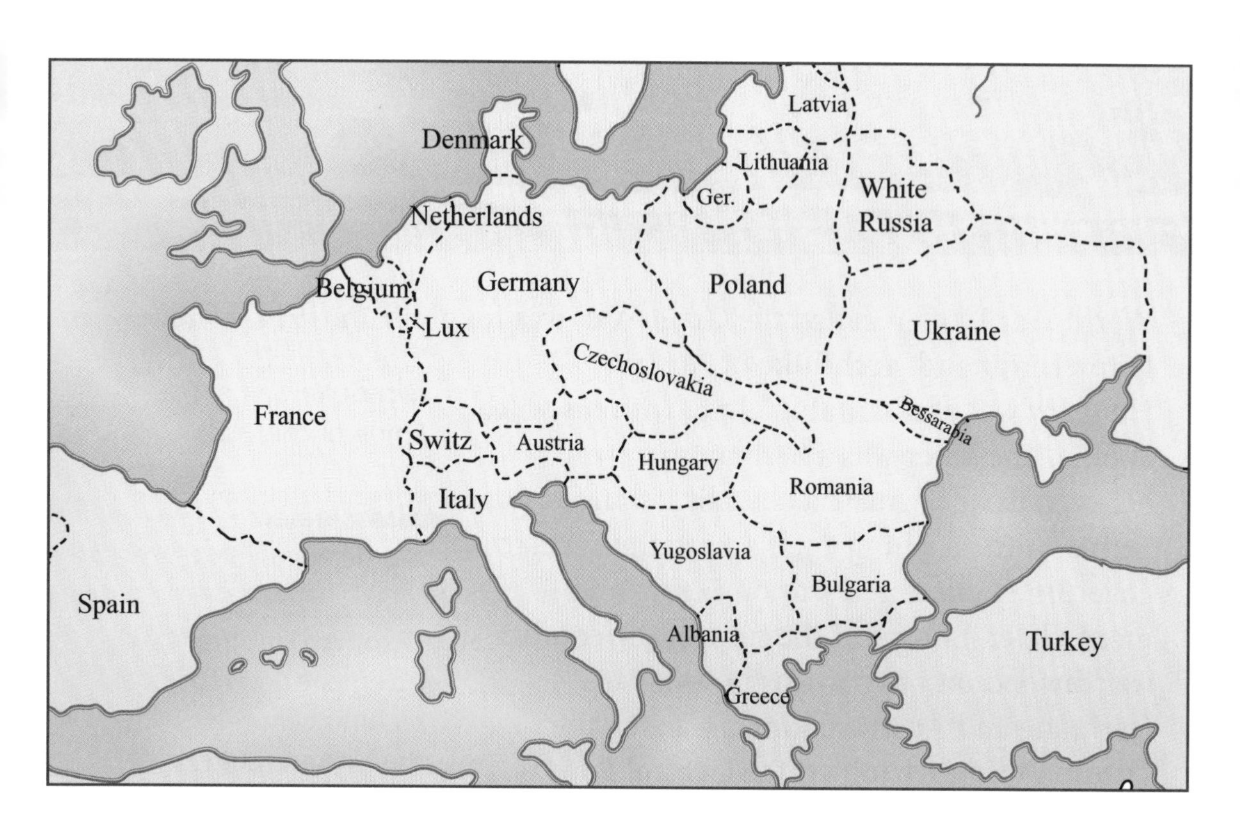

1

Murphy, the Donkey Who Carried the Wounded

April 1915– January 1916	Gallipoli, Turkey, World War I

The Battle of Gallipoli was fought during the First World War from April 25, 1915, to January 1916. It was the first major operation in which Allied forces arrived from the sea. British and French troops landed on the Turkish peninsula with **disastrous** consequences for the Allies. Half of the soldiers were either killed or wounded. The Turkish soldiers fought bravely to defend their homeland.

disastrous: Causing great damage

Jack Simpson Kirkpatrick

Jack Simpson Kirkpatrick grew up in South Shields, England. Twice during the year, there was a Fair at South Shields Market Place called Murphy's Fair. As a boy, Jack would spend his summer vacation working there, getting paid a **sixpence** a day, caring for the donkeys and giving children rides along the beach for a penny a ride. In the winter he delivered milk to help support his family of ten, as his father had suffered an injury and wasn't able to work. Whenever Jack found jobs, he gave most of the money he earned to his mother, whom he dearly loved.

sixpence: British money which was then worth 1/40th of their pound or 12.5 cents

He joined the **Merchant Marines** at age 17 and ended up in Australia. He was working as a fireman on a little coastal vessel in Western Australia when the war started. He enlisted in Perth, the capital of Western Australia, where

Merchant Marines: Civilians who transport troops and supplies in wartime on ships

for reasons not fully known, he enlisted as John Simpson, omitting his Scottish last name of Kirkpatrick. From then on, he was known as Simpson. He hoped joining up would enable him to return to England and his family soon. Like many who shared his reason for joining, Simpson was disappointed when the first Australian soldiers bound for the war were sent for training in Egypt.

Simpson had always loved animals, and from his first day in camp, he usually had a dog or two following him around. He also found a young possum and kept him as a pet while at camp, carrying it around in his hat and letting it sleep in his hammock with him at night. Simpson was strong and robust, so he was given the job of **stretcher bearer** in the 3rd Field Ambulance. It took a very strong man to be able to carry the weight of stretchers bearing wounded men. He was among those who landed at Gallipoli on April 25, 1915. At first, the stretcher-bearers were told to expect 3,000 wounded men at Gallipoli. That was soon changed to 10,000.

stretcher bearer: Person who carried the wounded on stretchers

On to Gallipoli

Arriving at the destination, Simpson climbed down a rope ladder into an overcrowded rowboat, silently praying they would not be killed. Enemy gunfire was heard as they rowed closer to the cliffs, which were covered with low trees and bushes. Simpson wished he was back home at good old South Shields.

He was the second man to get into the water and head for the beach. The first man and third man were killed beside him. Simpson felt a bullet whiz by his head as he waded toward an overhang to seek shelter. Soldiers swarmed onto the beach attempting to reach higher ground as they had been ordered. They clawed their way up steep slopes, using their bayonets to push themselves along and gain a foothold on the steep rocky banks. Enemy fire exploded overhead showering the area with **shrapnel**.

The 3rd **Brigade**, Simpson's squadron, captured the first of three ridges and chased the enemy inland, but having no **field artillery** in place, they suffered heavy losses. The guns had to be dragged up steep banks and were not yet there. Half the men were falling wounded and others were suffering from lack of food and water. Machine guns and shrapnel did much damage. The Turks had the advantage of having been there for months, plus they had many more men.

shrapnel: Fragments of a bomb or shell

brigade: Subdivision of an army

field artillery: Large guns used in warfare on land

evacuating: Removing from a place of danger

casualties: Persons injured in war

Simpson edged along narrow tracks, **evacuating** a steady stream of wounded men, and carrying them to lifeboats waiting along the shore. Stretchers became scarce as **casualties** mounted. "Shrapnel Gully," so named because of the constant barrage of shells flung down from the Turks, was the main highway to the front line. It was said this area was more dangerous than the actual **front line**. The stretcher-bearers did much of their work there. The cry of "stretcher-bearer" was heard from desperate wounded men, and respect grew daily for those who answered that cry and performed their miracles of bravery.

front line: Area closest to the conflict

A Donkey

On his second day after landing, Jack Simpson was reported missing, but actually, he was hard at work. He had come upon a donkey cowering in a grove of pines. Apparently, a few donkeys had been brought ashore with some mules to carry water to the men, but in the confusion of landing, some had been thrown out of the boats and left to swim to shore if they could make it. Jack, having a love for donkeys and prior experience with them, comforted the little fellow and named him "Murphy." Coming upon a wounded soldier, Simpson gently lifted the man onto Murphy's back, guiding the donkey with a lead rope he had improvised from field bandages. Murphy began to head down the stony **ravine** with his passenger. This was the first of many brave rescues. In rain or shine, Simpson was seen trudging up Shrapnel Gully with Murphy by his side. They made between 12 and 15 trips daily, carrying water to thirsty soldiers and coming back down with a wounded soldier **straddled** on Murphy's back. Simpson and Murphy were

ravine: Deep, narrow gorge with steep sides

straddled: One leg on each side

inseparable. Fearless for his own welfare, Jack Simpson was always considerate of his donkey.

One man recalls, "When the **enfilading** fire down the valley was at its worst and orders were posted that the ambulance men must not go out, the man and the donkey continued **placidly** at their work. At times they held trenches of hundreds of men **spellbound**, just to see them at their work. Their **quarry** lay motionless in an open patch, in easy range of a dozen Turkish rifles. Patiently, the little donkey waited under cover, while the man crawled through the thick scrub until he got within striking distance. Then a lightning dash, and he had the wounded man on his back and was making for cover again. In those fierce seconds, he always seemed to bear a life unusually protected from harm.

Once in cover, he tended to his **charge** with quick, skillful movements. Then the **limp** form was balanced across the back of the patient animal, and, with a slap on its back the man started off for the beach, the donkey trotting **unruffled** by his side."[1] Most of the wounded men were unable to walk, and Simpson was often seen holding an **unconscious** man with one arm while guiding the donkey with the other. Jack always had a smile and a word of encouragement for all.

enfilading: Bombarding

placidly: Steadily

spellbound: Curiously watching

quarry: Wounded victim

charge: Wounded man he was responsible for

limp: Helpless

unruffled: In a calm manner

unconscious: Passed out

At nighttime, Simpson often camped with an **Indian** artillery unit that named him *Bahadur*, meaning "Bravest of the Brave." They had the utmost respect for his bravery. The colonel of Simpson's squadron decorated Murphy's forehead with a red cross armband as he said to the donkey, "You're worth a hundred men to me."[2] **Padre** George Green said, "If ever a man deserved a **Victoria Cross** it was Jack Simpson. I often remember now the scene I frequently saw in Shrapnel Gully of that cheerful soul calmly walking down the **gully** with a red cross **armlet** tied round the donkey's head. That gully was under direct fire from the enemy almost all the time."[3]

Indian: Soldier from the country of India

padre: Minister

Victoria Cross: One of the highest awards for bravery a British soldier can receive

gully: Ravine formed by water

armlet: A band a medic would wear indicating his job as medic

Anzacs: Soldiers in the Australian and New Zealand Army Corps

barrage: Concentrated blast

The Last Trip for Simpson

In the middle of May, the Turks made their most violent attempt to drive the **Anzacs** and their Allies from the cliffs and send them back to the sea. There was a tremendous **barrage** of fire from their guns. They came across the narrow strip all together, rushing wildly, climbing over the sandbag lines only to die by enemy rifles. The battle raged on, but when it was finally over, it had failed. The Turks hadn't taken the trench. It was on the morning of this last attack, the 19th, that Simpson made his last journey. He went up for breakfast as usual, but it wasn't ready. Cheerfully, with a wave of his hand, he told the cook, "Never mind, get me a good dinner when I come back."[4]

Simpson set out with his donkey, as usual, to rescue more wounded men, as he did every other day. A Turkish soldier, taking careful aim, slowly squeezed the trigger. His target was a man leading a donkey up the steep incline at the junction of Dead Man's Ridge. Jack Simpson was struck in the back and the bullet passed through his heart, killing him instantly. Fellow soldiers dragged Jack off to the side. Andy Davidson, one of his friends, said, "We went back and covered his body and put it in a dugout by the side of the track and carried on with our job. We went back for him about 6:30 p.m., and he was buried at **Hell Spit** on that same evening."[5]

One of the other soldiers, when asked where Simpson was, answered that he was at Heaven's gate helping the soldiers through. The men had a hard time believing he was actually gone. Soldiers were teary-eyed as they watched Murphy trudging alone to the hospital station bearing his wounded cargo. Indian gunners, overcome with grief, risked their lives to collect a wreath of poppies to decorate a wooden cross. A hush had fallen over the camp.

Colonel John Monash wrote to Headquarters, New Zealand and Australian Division: "Private Simpson and his little beast earned the admiration of everyone at the upper end of the valley. They worked all day and night throughout the whole period since the landing, and the help **rendered** was invaluable. Simpson knew no fear and moved

Hell Spit: The most exposed part of the area held by Anzac troops

rendered: Given

unconcernedly amid shrapnel and rifle fire, steadily carrying out his **self-imposed** task day by day, and he frequently earned the applause of the personnel for his many fearless rescues of wounded men from the areas subject to rifle and shrapnel fire."[6]

How many lives Simpson and Murphy saved no one can say for sure, but it is estimated to be hundreds. Amazingly, it was done in less than the three weeks since they had landed.

So, what became of Murphy? Dale Collins and Dr. Charles Bean, Australia's official war correspondents and authors of Australian history books, both claim that Murphy became the pet of the 6th Mountain Battery Indians, who took him with them at the evacuation.

self-imposed: Job he had taken on himself

A letter was found written by the surgeon of an Indian Field Ambulance on Anzac, T.J. Carey Evans. He wrote that Murphy was evacuated to the safety of Mudros, a Greek island loaned to the Allies as a naval base so he would not be left to the mercy of the Turks. The letter also said that Murphy the donkey was well-known and liked among the Australians and the Indians who fought side by side. Carey Evans recalls a collar fastened on the donkey by the Australians on Mudros, reading: "Murphy VC — Please

look after him." They **speculate** that Murphy spent the rest of his days contentedly munching grass on the peaceful plains of the little island with memories of the kind man who adopted him, and with whom he walked the long, rough trail up and down Shrapnel Gully, saving many wounded men.

speculate: Have made an informed guess

There is a bronze statue of Jack Simpson and Murphy beside the Shrine of Remembrance in Melbourne, Australia. It's believed that Jack Simpson had at least one more donkey like Murphy that had been brought but abandoned, that he named "Duffy," and possibly others as well. He probably would give one a rest while using another. In 1997, Murphy was awarded a Purple Cross from the Royal Society for the Prevention of Cruelty to Animals (RSPCA), which is on display at the Australian War Memorial. A certificate they issued says: "… and for all the donkeys used by John Simpson Kirkpatrick, for the exceptional work they performed on behalf of humans while under continual fire at Gallipoli during World War I (1915)."

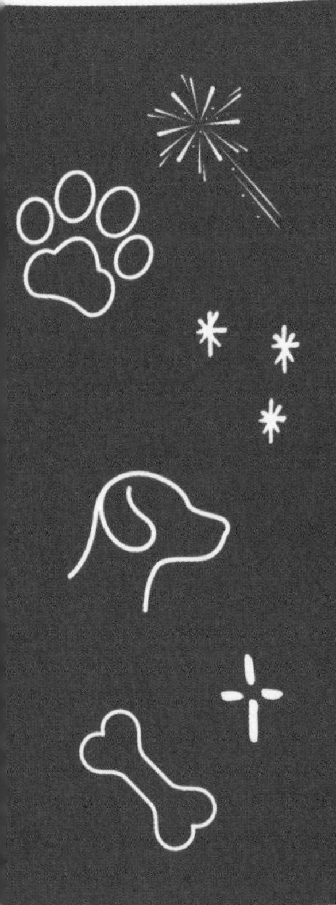

Sergeant Stubby, the Dog Who Caught a German Spy

1918	Third Battle of the Aisne, France, World War I

By the Third Battle of the Aisne, much of the world had been at war for three years. France, Great Britain, and Russia had been fighting with Germany and Austria-Hungary. The United States joined the Allied Powers only after Germany started attacking some American supply ships and tried to talk Mexico into going to war against the United States in exchange for land in the southwest part of the country. On April 6, 1917, America had officially joined the war.

Two Friends Meet

By summer of 1917, the Connecticut National Guard began training on the athletic grounds of Yale University. There, Robert Conroy, a 25-year-old private from New Britain, Connecticut, and Stubby became acquainted and soon became fast friends. No one seemed to know where Stubby, a brindle Boston bull terrier, had come from, but soon the soldiers found him hanging around the camp kitchen looking for scraps to eat. Stubby was exceptionally likable and intelligent, and all the men enjoyed having him around. He would visit soldiers in their tents, join them for military training exercises, and march in formation with the men. He definitely knew where all the **mess kitchens** were. It wasn't long before the friendly dog and the kind man found each other and became inseparable.

mess kitchens: Areas where meals are prepared for the soldiers

Moving Out

Robert taught Stubby many things, including how to **salute** by sitting down and rearing up on his hind legs while raising his paw to his forehead. At the end of the summer, change was about to come. Conroy's regiment was summoned to board a train for Norfolk, Virginia, where they would depart on the ship USS *Minnesota*, bound for Europe. There was one problem, though: dogs weren't allowed on board. Stubby didn't know that. He was bound and determined to follow his friend wherever he went. Robert and his fellow soldiers **formulated** a plan. They wrapped Stubby in a blanket, told him to be very quiet, and carried him up the **gangplank** into the vessel. There they hid poor Stubby in a coal bin in the ship's huge engine room until they were far enough out to sea that no one would even suggest sending the dog back. Stubby was a joy to the soldiers on the ship, reminding them of happier times back home with their families. During the voyage, Stubby would visit the **sentries**, join in ball games on deck, and snuggle up to many a soldier who was writing a letter home. At night, though, he would cuddle up to Robert in his bunk. Some soldiers who worked in the machine shop made Stubby a set of **dog tags** for his collar just like the men wore. They read, " 'STUBBY' 102nd INF, 26th Div."

salute: Make a formal hand gesture to display respect in military situations

formulated: Developed

gangplank: Movable plank used as a ramp to board or disembark from a ship

sentries: Soldiers stationed to keep guard

dog tags: Soldier's metal identity tags, usually worn on a chain around the neck

Arriving in France

At last, the journey was over. Fellow soldiers caused a friendly but noisy disturbance while Robert **stealthily** carried Stubby off ship in his blanket. Robert's commanding officer, however, suddenly spotted Stubby. Stubby immediately sat down, reared back on his **haunches**, and saluted the officer.

The CO was so amused and impressed that Stubby was not only allowed to stay but was proclaimed **mascot** of Conroy's unit. He was now an official member of the 102nd Infantry in the 26th Division, nicknamed the Yankee Division, as most of the men grew up in the New England states. They were among the first divisions to reach France from America, where they continued their training while waiting for more troops to arrive. Robert worked in the intelligence section. His unit was responsible for learning and transporting information for a regiment of 3,700 men. When Robert was carrying messages to other outfits, Stubby trotted beside the horse Robert was riding. When Robert stood guard, Stubby was faithfully by his side.

stealthily: Secretly and quietly

haunches: Fleshy hindquarters of an animal

mascot: Animal kept to strengthen the morale of soldiers

The Front Lines

It was February 5, 1918, when the Yankee Division reached the front lines of northeastern France at a place called **Chemin des Dames**. It was the job of the American soldiers to keep the Germans from breaking through French **fortifications** that were protecting the capital city of Paris. The French front lines were a series of interconnecting **trenches** dug into the ground. Sometimes the men had to sleep in the mud and dirt. Between the German and French lines was an open field called "No Man's Land," because no man wanted to get caught out there without the protection of the trenches.

Chemin des Dames: Ladies Road

fortifications: Defensive walls built to strengthen against attack

trenches: Long, deep ditches used as protective defenses

Stubby soon learned the difference between the sound of French and German guns. He heard the sound of approaching shells long before the men did, alerting them by barking furiously. Dogs have a keener sense of smell than humans, and he forewarned the men of the invading smell of poison gas coming their way, so they had time to grab their gas masks and put them on for protection. Stubby had his own gas mask that Robert would put on him when the danger came. Sensing an attack, he would run through the trenches barking to warn his soldier friends. Stubby also helped the men by killing many rats that swarmed through the camp and trenches.

Wounded

On April 20, 1918, the enemy attacked the Allied lines. Heavy fighting took place. Finally, as the battle progressed, the German **assault** collapsed, and they began to **retreat**. When the shelling quieted down, Stubby ventured out of the trench to check the battlefield for wounded men. Suddenly a shell exploded, and shrapnel lodged in his chest. When Stubby howled, Robert crawled from the trenches and rescued him. He was hurt badly, but Robert did his best to patch him up until he could get him to the regiment's doctor.

assault: Attack in battle

retreat: Withdraw

Stubby was put into an ambulance with wounded soldiers and went off as Robert watched. An army surgeon removed the shrapnel and stitched and bandaged Stubby's wound. Robert and his buddies worried a lot about their furry friend. "For days there was deep gloom in the outfit lest Stubby should not get well."[7] Six weeks later, they were reunited, and the men learned that Stubby had fully recovered. They also learned Stubby had cheered the men laid up in the hospital while he was there.

Back to Work

It was June before Stubby could rejoin the 102nd regiment. Conroy and Stubby continued delivering messages between Allied forces and gathering information about the enemy's movements. Shortly after

Stubby returned, they were on the move again. The **Second Battle of the Marne** was about to start. The Allies left their trenches. Fighting took place in big open wheat fields. Many men were killed or wounded. That's when Stubby took on a new role. He began to find wounded men who had fallen and were hidden from sight by waist-high wheat. He would alert medics to their location. Stubby knew the difference between Americans and Germans by their uniforms and how they talked. If Stubby sensed a man was dying, he would snuggle up next to him in his last moments. He brought comfort to many. Many Germans were surrendering. Robert would talk to them to get information; Stubby would make sure they didn't try to sneak away while being led to prison.

Second Battle of the Marne: An offensive during World War I by the British and French forces

disinfected: Chemical removal of bacteria

Stubby Gets a Jacket

In early August, the 26th Division earned a little break from fighting. The men were able to take much-needed baths, and get their clothes cleaned and **disinfected**, as they had been too engaged in fighting to be able to bathe. Stubby and his unit had helped liberate the French town of Chateau-Thierry, and now many local women sewed Stubby a jacket out of tough chamois leather. It fastened under his neck with decorative buttons, and snaps closed it shut on his stomach. They sewed braided cord onto the coat, writing "Stubby" and "102nd U.S. INF" on the left side. They even made a colorful **emblem** out of silk thread for the back of his coat. They made it to show their appreciation for his efforts in **liberating** their town.

Capturing a German Spy

In early September, the 26th Division helped clear Germans from the area around St. Mihiel, France, capturing 15,000 soldiers in four days! The Yankee Division then joined what the Allied commanders hoped would be the last operation of the war: the **Meuse-Argonne campaign**. Half a million soldiers secretly moved into positions along the 30-mile battlefront.

emblem: Badge

liberating: Freeing

Meuse-Argonne campaign: Largest operation of the American Expeditionary Forces in World War I

What was supposed to be over in a few days lasted more than six weeks. Rains caused much mud, and soldiers had to eat cold food. The shelling seemed unbearable. The men never got much rest. It was during this time that Stubby accomplished what was probably his most outstanding wartime achievement. He captured a German spy! Stubby spotted the man and somehow recognized him as not being a member of their

division. Dogs have very sensitive noses, and the spy most likely gave off a scent that would alert a dog to danger. Stubby barked a loud alarm to alert his men. When the man attempted to run away, Stubby knocked him down and bit the seat of the soldier's pants, holding on until help came. The Americans discovered the man had written details of their camp that would have significantly helped the enemy. Stubby earned high praise for this tremendous act. Stubby was given the rank of sergeant. He even was permitted to keep the German spy's **Iron Cross** as a reward for capturing the spy. "To the victor goes the **spoils**," said one of the soldiers as he handed the Iron Cross to Robert, who then pinned it to Stubby's new coat.[8]

The Final Attack

It was mid-October when the commanders in charge stopped the Meuse-Argonne assaults and began to regroup troops for one final attack. The Yankee Division's job was to distract the Germans on the flank and keep them from moving reinforcements to the middle of the front line. That is where the Allies were planning to launch their attack. The ground the Germans held was known as the Hindenburg Line. It consisted of three long bands of trenches that covered 12 miles behind No Man's Land, which the Germans had held since 1914, so they were well-established. The Americans began to gain ground; then they would lose ground, only to gain it again. The men of the Yankee Division were hungry and tired, but they continued to push on, making progress slowly but surely. The Germans constantly were bombing the Americans with gas shells.

Iron Cross: Highest German military decoration for bravery

spoils: Plunder

Some of the chemicals made breathing hard, some caused temporary blindness, and others made men break out in painful blisters.

On November 2, one of the shells came so fast that Stubby had time to bark a warning, but Robert couldn't get his mask or Stubby's on fast enough. Both man and dog struggled to breathe and had to be taken to a nearby Army hospital to recover. When they returned to duty, it was only a question of when the Germans would surrender. The Allies, although losing many men, had been able to drive 43 German divisions back about 30 miles over some of the most difficult terrain and most heavily fortified positions on the Western Front. The war was drawing to a close.

Cease Fire

On Sunday, November 10, the rumor was that an **armistice** would happen in the morning at 11 o'clock. Both Allies and Axis powers told their men to use up all the ammo with one last push to continue taking ground. The noise of the guns was deafening. Then, all of a sudden, at 11 a.m., there was silence. "The silence is oppressive. It weighs in on one's eardrums," one soldier wrote in his diary.[9] Immediately, soldiers left their trenches and celebrations began. Many soldiers gathered around Stubby, congratulating him for all his help in obtaining victory. Former enemies met in No Man's Land, swapping souvenirs and helping each other locate the dead from both sides. Even though they had lost the war, most

armistice:
Agreement made by opposing sides in a war to stop fighting for a certain time

Germans were so happy that the war was over, and they could go home. One of the Yankee Division soldiers wrote a poem about Stubby and read it to all the men at an **impromptu** victory celebration. Robert whispered to Stubby, "You're coming home with me, Stubby. If I have to, I'll sneak you on a ship like I did before."[10]

The soldiers soon learned going home wouldn't be a fast process. They settled into postwar camps while arrangements were made.

When President Woodrow Wilson visited the Yankee Division on Christmas Day 1918, he met Stubby and shook his paw. Stubby received wound stripes and service bars for his uniform, along with all the soldiers. The French gave the soldiers medals to thank them for their participation in liberating France. Robert made sure Stubby received his too. His jacket was adorned with red ribbon from Verdun, gold and red ribbon for St. Mihiel, and white ribbon for Chateau-Thierry, along with a commemorative award hung from a peppermint-striped ribbon given by the French government. Each Allied nation also issued its own victory medal. Stubby's victory medal included five crossbars to identify where he had fought: Champagne-Marne, Aisne-Marne, St. Mihiel, Meuse-Argonne, and the "Defensive Sector." Stubby was credited with participation in 17 battles. People honored Stubby as a hero dog.

impromptu: Unplanned

Home at Last

Robert came down with the Spanish flu, a **potentially** deadly virus that had killed many during the war. Stubby was allowed to stay with him as he recovered at a local hospital. When Robert Conroy's ship finally landed in Boston Harbor, friends, relatives, and the governors of three states greeted them. Some 20,000 soldiers of the Yankee Division marched through the streets of Boston in a victory parade. More than a million people cheered them on. Stubby walked in a place of honor with the 102nd regiment.

potentially: Possibly

Stubby lived with Robert for the rest of his life. Post-war, his fame continued to grow, and he met three presidents: Woodrow Wilson, Calvin Coolidge, and Warren G. Harding. General John J. Pershing pinned a gold medal on him given by the American Humane Society. Even as he aged, he attended dog shows and veteran fundraising events, had his portrait painted, and participated in charity events and parades. Stubby never tired of being around old Army soldiers.

He remained devoted to Robert and died peacefully in Robert's arms at 12 years of age. Robert had preserved Stubby's body after his death. It now abides in the Smithsonian Museum in Washington, D.C., along with his brass-studded collar, his leather harness, and his highly decorated jacket, located in "The Price of Freedom" exhibit. Books have been written about Stubby. His story still inspires young and old today.

SERGEANT STUBBY
HERO DOG OF WWI
A BRAVE STRAY

3

Cher Ami, the Pigeon Who Saved the Lost Battalion

October 1918	Argonne Forest in France, World War I

The **Argonne Forest** was located in northeast France. It was the Germans' main **defensive** position ever since 1914. The forest was ten miles wide, consisting of hills, thick woods, and massive underbrush. It was defended by German machine gunners who had built trenches. **Snipers** and **land mines** were thick throughout the forest. The Allies felt they needed to capture the railway hub at **Sedan** to keep supplies from getting to the Germans. However, the Argonne Forest stood in the way. It was decided to plan an assault on September 25 with a 24-hour artillery bombardment which dropped 40,000 tons of explosives on the German lines — more shells than all the cannon ammunition fired by the Union Army in the Civil War.

General of the Armies John Joseph Pershing was a senior United States Army officer. He served most famously as the commander of the American Expeditionary Forces on the Western Front during World War I, from 1917 to 1918. "The assault of 26 September," Pershing wrote later, "surprised the Germans and disrupted their defense, but this situation was only momentary. From that day on the fighting was probably **unsurpassed** during the

Argonne Forest: Long strip of mountainous and wild woodland in northeastern France

defensive: Being prepared to attack or defend

snipers: Riflemen who fire from concealed places

land mines: Underground mines that exploded when vehicles or troops passed over them

Sedan: A city that was a crucial supply center located approximately 80 miles northeast of Paris

unsurpassed: Never done better

World War for dogged determination on both sides." That was Pershing looking back calmly on the situation long after the war. At the time his opening drive was stopped on October 1, however, he was too furious to praise the determination of his tired troops. He ordered them to get moving forward again the next day "without regard of losses and without regard to the exposed conditions of the flanks (side)...."[11]

Major Whittlesey, formerly a successful New York lawyer, was chosen to lead the assault. He commanded the 1st Battalion, 308th Infantry, 154th Brigade, 77th Division of the American Expeditionary Forces. His unit was made up mostly of men from the state of New York.

The men charged hard, but the Germans responded with a fierce counterattack that took a heavy toll on his men. Nevertheless, Whittlesey's men managed to break into the Argonne and overrun German positions. At the end of the first day, the Allied **offensive** came to a halt so the men could get much-needed rest. During the next five days, they didn't make much progress, as the Germans had regrouped and managed to hold their ground.

offensive: Attack

The Attack

On the evening of October 1, Major Whittlesey was given orders to lead an attack the following morning. He was expected to break through German lines and **dig in** above Charlevaux Brook and there await further orders. He begged for more supplies and **rations** for his exhausted men, who were down to half-strength now. He felt it would be close to impossible to hazard that rough terrain. He was promised support by the 307th Infantry as well as a French unit.

It was early on the morning of October 2 when they set out and at first encountered no German resistance. Suddenly, the German machine gunners began to open fire upon them. Whittlesey sent word to the commanding officer, Colonel Stacy, saying his men were like **sitting ducks** and could advance no farther. Word was sent back that they must proceed and take Hill 198. He saw no evidence of the 307th or a French unit coming to assist, but orders were orders, and they must be obeyed. When Stacy passed the order on to Whittlesey, the major saluted and said, "All right. I'll attack, but whether you'll hear from me again, I don't know."[12]

dig in: Create a defensive position by digging foxholes or trenches

rations: Alloted amounts

sitting ducks: Easy targets

The men located a German machine gun nest that was instrumental in firing upon them and were able to put it out of action. They had actually taken Hill 198! "The Americans learned later that the fortifications on Hill 198 had been manned by older enemy soldiers, men in their late 40s and early 50s, who had been without food for two days. Most of them had deserted their posts during the morning's bombardment."[13] The Americans then pushed on beyond

Charlevaux Brook and set up a defensive position which became known as the Pocket. Advancing so rapidly, however, left the unit unprotected on its flanks. They were in danger of being surrounded by the enemy. The Germans in the Argonne Forest had lines of telephone communication, but Whittlesey's unit did not. To get a message back to his regimental command post, Whittlesey used a team of **runners**, posted at intervals in the woods. Major Whittlesey immediately sent a runner to inform Colonel Stacy of his position. When the Germans learned the American troops had broken through the lines, they turned every available soldier to oppose them.

Trapped

Daybreak on October 3 found the 77th Division surrounded on both flanks. The Germans retook Hill 198 behind them. No more runners could get through. It seemed hopeless. They were trapped in the Pocket. There was one hope left. Omer Richards, a French Canadian private from upstate New York who was the caretaker of the First Battalion's pigeons, had carried a cage with eight birds during the advance through the enemy line. Pigeons were known to be fast fliers and were invaluable in World War I, as they were used to deliver messages. Six hundred carrier pigeons were trained and used during World War I. They had been trained to fly to command posts with folded notes attached to a tiny metal canister fastened to their legs.

runners: Foot soldiers responsible for carrying messages between units during war

Upon landing they were rewarded with food. They could travel up to 50 miles per hour.

Whittlesey sent two messages by pigeons stating his exact location and requesting reinforcements and artillery support. The Germans had **targeted** their position and they needed help quickly. His men were hungry; many were severely wounded, and many had been killed. No help came. The Germans knew about the pigeons and, of course, watched for them, and targeted them. Desperately, two more pigeons were sent but were also shot down.

October 4 came, and the Germans were closer still. Whittlesey sent the fifth pigeon asking for immediate help. Major General Alexander, who was responsible for the mission, had desperately been trying to locate the 77th. He even sent aircraft to look for the men, but to no avail. Then the 5th pigeon arrived. At 2:30 p.m., a U.S. **artillery regiment** began to **bombard** the German forces near Whittlesey's location. The men were thrilled. Help was on the way!

targeted: Shot at

artillery regiment: Soldiers who provide indirect fire in support of military maneuvers

bombard: Attack with bombs, shells, or missiles

Suddenly, though, the bombs began to fall on the American men of the 77th. Their own men were bombarding them now! Inaccurate coordinates had been mistakenly written down and delivered by the fifth pigeon. The American artillery gunners thought they were bombing the Germans. The wounded were taken to cover, and the men began to pray, fearing they would all be killed. Whittlesey desperately wrote a message saying, "We are along the road parallel 276.4. Our own artillery is dropping a barrage directly on us. For heaven's sake stop it. — Whittlesey."[14]

Their Last Hope

There was only one bird left to send. His name was Cher Ami — their very last hope and their favorite bird. He was released and German riflemen immediately fired upon him. Whittlesey had no idea if Cher Ami would make it or not, but the men were all praying he would. Cher Ami was hit in his chest as the Germans continued to blast away, and he was badly wounded. The soldiers watched in alarm as he stopped moving and fell to the ground.

Then suddenly, Cher Ami struggled up to fly again. He had not given up! It seemed incredible! As the men watched, he flapped his wings and took off again to try to complete his mission as he'd been trained to do. He pressed on for 25 miles despite his wounds. A half hour later, he made it! Cher Ami had saved 194 men of the 77th! The artillery unit was notified immediately to **cease** firing on their own men. As the bombing stopped, the men of the 77th began cheering and praising faithful little Cher Ami who had come through for them again! Months earlier the brave bird had delivered 12

cease: Stop

important messages at the Battle of Verdun. Cher Ami in French means "dear friend," and certainly Cher Ami was a dear friend to the men of the 77th. On October 7, the men of the 77th were finally rescued. Of the 687 men who began the mission, 500 had been killed or wounded. The newspapers called them "The Lost Battalion," and a movie was even made about them.

What Happened to Cher Ami?

And what had happened to Cher Ami? Arriving at his home loft, he lay still as a stone. He was covered in blood from the hole in his chest, blinded in one eye, and what was left of his left leg was dangling at his side, but he had managed to deliver the life-giving message! Quickly, an army veterinarian attended to Cher Ami's wounds. He was able to save his life, but not his leg. One of the soldiers carved him a new leg from a tree branch as Army medics worked to save his life. When he recovered enough to travel, the now one-legged bird was put on a boat to the United States, with General John J. Pershing seeing him off. He returned home to America in April 1919. Cher Ami became the hero of the 77th Infantry Division and a hero to all Americans.

Cher Ami was awarded the French Cross of War, a high honor given to soldiers in combat. The story of the brave pigeon who saved the Lost Battalion was all over the newspapers, and the story of Cher Ami was known by American school children of the 1920s and 1930s. Cher Ami was as well-known as any human World War I hero. In 1931, Cher Ami was **inducted** into the Racing Pigeon Hall of Fame and given a gold medal for outstanding service during World War I. In November 2019, he became one of the first winners of the Animals in War & Peace Medal of Bravery, bestowed on him **posthumously** at a ceremony on Capitol Hill in Washington, D.C. Cher Ami was born in April 1918, and died on June 13, 1919, the date that later would become known as International Pigeon Appreciation Day. His body was preserved and put on display at the Smithsonian Institute in June 1921. Cher Ami is currently on display at the National Museum of History and Technology at the Smithsonian. Should you have the opportunity to go to see

inducted: Formally admitted

posthumously: After he had died

that museum in Washington D.C., be sure to stop by and say hello to the courageous pigeon who was willing to sacrifice and endure hardship to save the lives of the men of the Lost Battalion.

The Alaskan Black Death

Diphtheria was a disease that people called the "black death" because it killed those infected with it. It was highly **contagious**, which is why certain doctors wore masks that looked like a bird's face to protect them from breathing in the sickness. At the start of the year 1925, a breakout of the disease occurred in Nome, Alaska, a small town not far south of the Arctic Circle. Nome was far from any other towns, and Alaska was in the dead of winter, making travel by land or sea near impossible due to the heavy ice and snow. How

contagious: Easily spread from one person to another

were the people of Nome going to survive without diphtheria medicine? There was only one solution: dog sleds! In a feat of bravery, perseverance, and self-sacrifice, both men and canines risked their lives in a trip known as the Great Race of Mercy to deliver a life-saving medicine to the inhabitants of Nome.

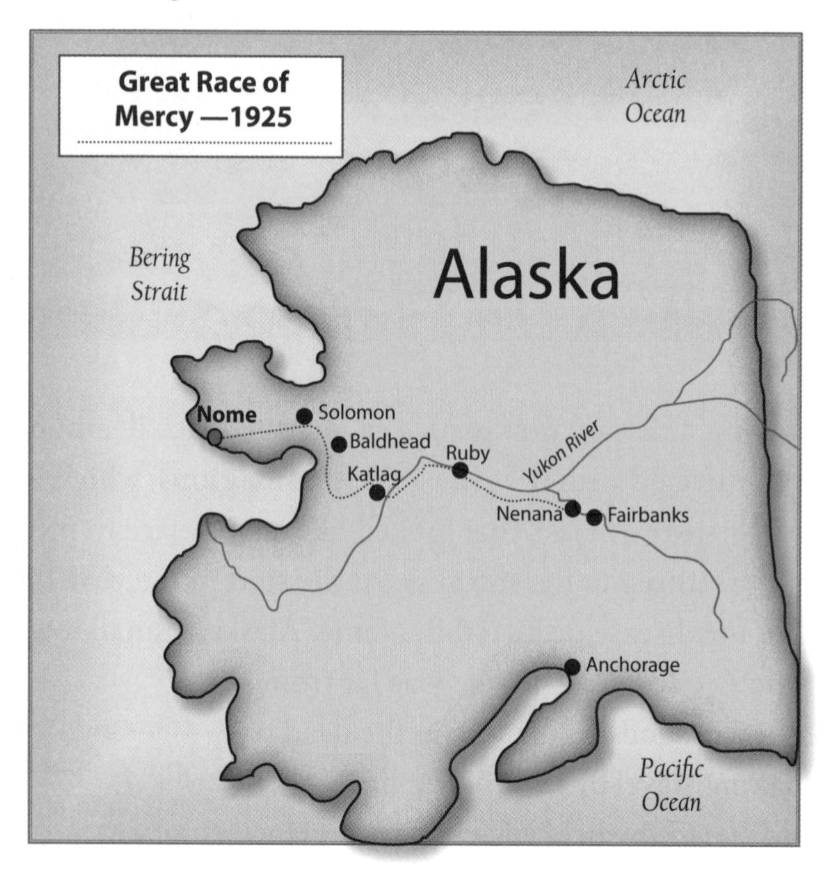

4

Balto—The Dog Who Saved Nome

January–February 1925	Nome, Alaska

It was January 1925. Dr. Curtis Welch, the family doctor of a small town called Nome, made a **house call** to the home of two small **Inuit** children. "There has not been a case of diphtheria in this area for 20 years. I must be wrong," Dr. Welch thought.[15] But he soon learned he was right when the children died, and more were getting sick. Diphtheria medicine was needed, and it was needed quickly. Something must be done before it infected all the people in Nome.

Help Is Requested

Dr. Welch immediately sent out a radio signal from Nome across Alaska: "We need diphtheria **serum**. The 'black death' is here!" Doctors in Anchorage heard the signal and responded that they had 3,000 units of the needed serum, which was enough to save the children's lives and prevent an epidemic. Now the problem arose of how to get it to Nome. They could send it by train to the town of Nenana, but that was as far as the railroad went. Nenana lay close to 700 miles away from Nome, and those miles were covered by snow and ice. Snow was falling heavily, and the temperature was dropping steadily.

house call: When the doctor visits the home instead of the patient going to the hospital

Inuit: Indigenous people of Alaska

serum: Medicine made up of antibodies

A Possible Solution

The mayor of Nome told Dr. Watson that the mail carriers followed a trail from Nenana to Nome, but it took a mail carrier almost 30 days to travel that road, and that would be too long. More and more people would die by then. Dogs were the only possible answer! There was an experienced team of **mushers** who ran the **Iditarod Trail**.

Relay teams were selected so rested drivers could be waiting at every station to get the serum and take it by dogsled to the next stop, where another man would be waiting. This way no time would be lost, and the hope was to have the serum delivered to Nome in 15 days. Dr. Watson was afraid many people would die before then, but that was the best they could do. A radio message went out over the airways asking for volunteer dog sled drivers and their teams to help with the rescue project. Many teams were needed, and they needed the best and fastest teams available to save as many lives as possible.

mushers: Drivers of dog sleds

Iditarod Trail: Longest annual sled dog race in the world

relay: Each member travels a certain distance and passes the medicine to the next team

lead dogs: Dogs placed at the head of the team, who were skilled in following the trail and leading the other dogs in the pack

Volunteers Respond

Men responded from little villages all along the trail from Nenana to Nome. The drivers got their teams ready. In the early 1900s, the only way to travel across Alaska's deep winter snow was by dogsled. Dogs who were the most intelligent were chosen to be **lead dogs**. When the drivers wanted the teams to start, they would shout the command, "Mush!" as a signal for the dogs to begin.

In Nome, a man named Leonhard Seppala and his friend Gunnar Kaasen worked for a gold mining company. They had a team of dogs trained to haul food and tools from Nome to the gold camp several miles away. The two men kept busy training their dog team. Sometimes on a trip, they would find someone who had hunted a moose for food, who asked them to haul the meat back to Nome for him. Often, if a person became sick, the dogs pulled him on a sled to Dr. Watson, Nome's only doctor. In summertime, the team was hitched to a small flatcar that ran on an old railroad track and would transport gold miners who wanted to get to town. The gold miners nicknamed this type of transportation their "pupmobile." Here is where a dog named Balto, a husky, was trained to be on a dogsled team.

Leonhard Seppala was now asked to go to the station at Nulato, the halfway point along the trail. Kaasen needed to stay behind to haul food to the gold camp. There were 33 dogs in their kennel. Seppala chose Togo as his lead dog. The dogs were hitched to the sled and Seppala shouted the command, "Mush!" The excited dogs began to run. Meanwhile, people at Nenana were awaiting the arrival of the train.

Bill Shannon was to be the first musher. His team was ready when, at midnight, the train carrying the precious 20-pound package of serum arrived. Shannon tied the package to his sled and off they went, as people watching cried, "Good luck!" When he started out, the temperature was 30 degrees below zero and then it began to steadily drop: -35, -40, -45, and then -50 degrees below zero. The doctor had given instructions to warm the serum at each stop to keep it from freezing. The race was on — a race of men and dogs against time and cold.

The Race Is On

Fifty-two miles later, Shannon handed the serum to Edgar Kalland, who ran his team to the next stop. Each man passed the serum to the next man. When Charlie Evans was making his run, two of his dogs froze to death. Evans strapped his own body to the sled and helped the dogs pull to the next stop. Brave men waited at each stop along the way, ready to join in this race against time. Finally, the halfway point was reached. Seppala, with his Siberian husky Togo, raced down the trail, braving cracking ice around the dangerous Norton Sound. He completed the longest and hardest stretch of all — 91 miles.

Back in Nome, the sky turned dark, a sign that a storm was on the way, a bad one. The mayor decided that more mushers were needed so they could have shorter runs. That way, the men and dogs braving the oncoming storm wouldn't be in danger of freezing. But there was no time to send out another message. Only one experienced musher remained in Nome — Gunnar Kaasen. He would be the one to help Charlie Olson and Ed Rohn on the last two runs, making three teams instead of two when the storm would be at its worst.

Balto Gets Ready

Kaasen lost no time in dressing warmly and heading to the kennel. Balto leaped with excitement when he realized Kaasen was choosing him as lead dog. He had never been the lead dog before. The husky ran to his place at the front of the line. They headed to Bluff, the station where they would await the arrival of Charlie Olson and the life-giving serum. They were still waiting the next day as the storm began to turn into a full-fledged blizzard. Despite Kaasen's hopes that Olson could make it, fighting the storm had slowed Olson down, and it was night before he finally arrived. Kaasen hurried out to meet him.

Olson's dogs were close to frozen as Kaasen helped him get them to safety and warmed the serum. "Kaasen, you can't drive in this weather. The wind must be blowing 50 miles an hour. You will have to wait until the storm is over," said Olson.[16] Kaasen knew that wind makes cold even colder, but he also knew people were dying in Nome, and every minute counted. The mushers had gotten the serum this far — 600 miles in only five days. "I'm not going to stop the relay now," he decided.[17] He knew Ed Rohn would be waiting at Point Safety to take the serum on the last leg of the trip.

It was more than 50 degrees below zero and winds were gale-force, cutting sharply as they whipped around man and dog. As Kaasen slipped the lead harness over Balto's dark head, his ears pricked forward and his intelligent eyes gleamed. He was chosen! Today he would face his first great test. Kaasen, in his heavy coat and woolen mittens, tied the serum to the sled and hitched up all 13 dogs. As he snapped the lead on Balto, he knelt and looked into the husky's big eyes. "I'm counting on you, Balto," he said.[18] Kaasen had always favored Balto from the time he was a pup and saw his great potential to be a lead dog all through his training. Olson begged him not to attempt it, but Kaasen's mind was made up. "Mush!" he shouted, and into the howling storm they went.

Night of Danger

At first, the trail had a crust of ice on it, so the dogs found it easy to run. Soon, however, they came to a spot with drifted snow, and the dogs sank to their stomachs and couldn't move. Kaasen took hold of Balto's collar, and he and Balto pulled and tugged with all their might. Slowly, they led the helpless team out of danger. A few miles later, Balto came to a sudden halt. "What's wrong?" Kaasen shouted. Then he

understood — they had been crossing a frozen river, but water was coming up through a crack in the ice. Balto was standing in a pool of water, but he had stopped before the team was in danger. Kaasen knew he had to act quickly. If a dog's feet froze, he would never walk again. Kaasen found a patch of snow and quickly unhitched Balto, leading him to the patch. Balto understood what he must do and rubbed his feet in the powdery snow until they were dry. Soon he was ready to go on. "Good boy!" Kaasen told him. Balto had saved them all from an icy grave.

Next, they reached a high, steep hill. Kaasen wasn't sure the dogs could climb up such an icy slope. But Balto climbed, pulling with all his might as Kaasen pushed from behind. Slowly, they made it up the hill. Balto gave his tail one happy wag and on they went. The next challenge was a long icy stretch that was extremely slick. Kaasen was hoping the storm would die down before they had to brave this stretch of the path, but instead, it picked up speed. Snow blinded them as the wind cut like knives. The blizzard was bearing down heavily upon them! It was so thick that Kaasen couldn't see the dog ahead of him! He couldn't even see his raised hand in front of him. The snow was like a curtain surrounding them. Kaasen knew if he couldn't see, then neither could Balto. There was nothing Kaasen could do but trust the **instincts** of his lead dog.

instincts: Capability to automatically know how to behave or respond in certain circumstances

Suddenly, the sled twisted sideways, sliding off the trail into the Topkok River! Kaasen fell but got back up, helping Balto get the sled upright again. With the storm still raging, Kaasen **marveled** at how the dog was able to smell out the trail in such a blizzard. At last, the storm began to die down and the dreadful run was almost over. Point Safety lay just ahead!

The Last Run

When they reached Point Safety, the cabin was dark, and no musher team awaited them. Kaasen decided not to stop to find out what had happened. They learned later that Ed Rohn had blown out the light and gone to bed, assuming there was no way Kaasen would have braved the blizzard, or that if he had, he would have frozen to death. Kaasen and his team would have to carry the precious medicine twice as far. He could hardly move his legs, and his dogs were slowing down. Kaasen felt all the dogs' paws, **assessing** if they could continue. Two dogs were almost freezing, so he covered them in rabbit skin blankets. Kaasen finished caring for the dogs and, though extremely weary, they pressed on. Winds **accelerated** as they plowed ahead.

Suddenly a gust of wind lifted the dogs and sled into the air, **hurling** them into a snowdrift. The huskies landed in a tangle of harness and fur. Balto hesitated, seeing that Kaasen was on

marveled: Filled with wonder

assessing: Determining

accelerated: Got stronger

hurling: Throwing

his knees, frantically searching in the snow. The serum was gone — after safely making it this far. He had to find it! Lives depended on it. Finally, with fingers stiff from the cold snow, Kaasen retrieved the package from the drift, got the dogs untangled, and they were off again.

There at Last

"At 5:30 a.m. on February 2, Kaasen and his team, staggering and frozen to the bone, drove past the silent streets and wooden house fronts of Nome. They had made most of the run in total darkness."[19] They had come 53 miles through an intense blizzard against all odds. Soon families of the sick children would awake and crowd around them with tears in their eyes, knowing their children would live. Kaasen gave a huge hug to Balto, who had brought them through somehow. The serum had arrived in only five and half days from Nenana — in time to save Nome! The spread of the sickness was stopped and there were no more deaths.

The Alaskan people honored all the mushers and dogs involved in the relay, but Balto was esteemed as the greatest hero of all. Newspapers in the United States printed the story. Magazines carried his picture. In New York, a beautiful bronze statue of Balto still stands in Central Park. The strong black husky had become one of the most famous dogs in the world! For the rest of his life, Balto led Gunnar Kaasen's teams. They were good friends and partners, working together at the job they loved best, and America was ever thankful for Balto — the dog who helped save Nome.

World War II took place between 1939–1945 and was the largest and deadliest war in history. This time, the Allied Powers included the United States, Britain, the Soviet Union, and the Free French. Germany, Italy, and Japan joined to form the Axis Powers. There were many contributing factors to World War II, including wars between Italy and Ethiopia, China, and Japan; conflicts between the Soviet Union, Mongolia, and Japan; the rise of **fascism** in Europe; and tension in Europe following the First World War. The

fascism: A belief that nation and race are more important than anything else; often resulting in an all-powerful, oppressive government

Second World War officially began when Germany invaded Poland in September 1939, after which both Britain and France declared war on Germany. As the war progressed, conflict and captures took place in many other **theaters**, including areas near the islands of Indonesia, such as the British island of Singapore and the Territory of New Guinea.

theaters: Areas of important military events

culminating: Ending

unforgiving: Extremely difficult

In 1943, the Allies invaded Sicily, Italy, forcing the Axis Powers to retreat. This was no small victory, but Axis forces still had control of Italy. At the Battle of Monte Cassino, the plan was to capture Italy's capital, Rome. However, the terrain there was **unforgiving**, making the soldiers' objective grueling and dangerous. Many more battles were fought as the war neared an end, **culminating** in the collapse of the Axis Powers and an Allied victory in September 1945.

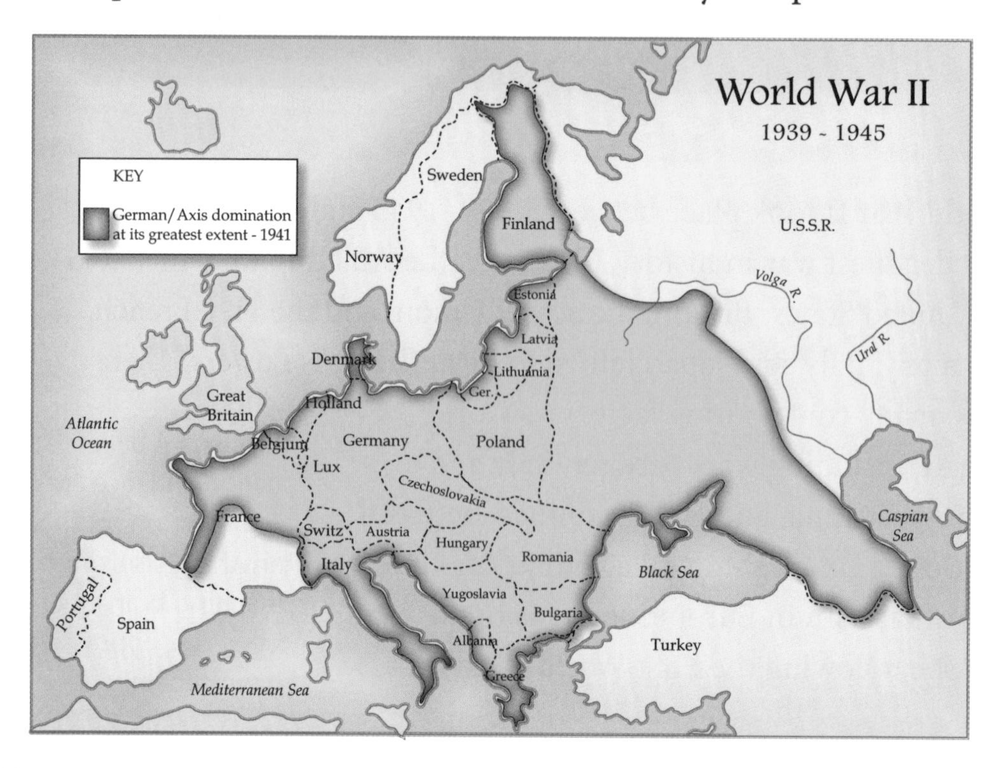

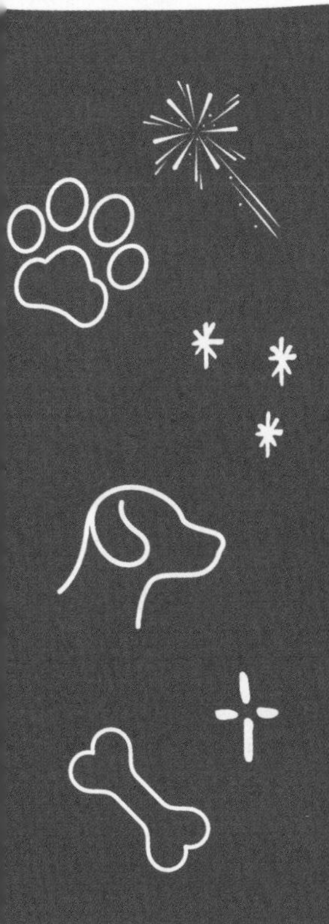

5

Tipperary Beauty, the Dog Who Rescued Pets

1940	The Blitz, London, World War II

When France surrendered in June 1940, Germany turned its fury on its next target — Great Britain. On August 2, 1940, Hitler issued a plan of attack, ordering massive airstrikes that would destroy British air power and open the way for a land invasion of England. The intense bombing campaign was called the Blitz, derived from the German word, "**blitzkrieg**." For eight months, the **Luftwaffe** dropped bombs on London and other British cities. It became known as the Battle of Britain.

The Blitzkrieg

Germany's attempted invasion of Britain began in September 1940. Ear-piercing air raid sirens signaling that bomber planes were approaching would sound to alert the British people to drop what they were doing and run to bomb shelters. People stayed in the shelters until an "all-clear" signal sounded. In London, at the peak of the Blitz, about 150,000 people took shelter nightly in underground stations. Night after night, cities across the country became targets. Make-shift **air-raid** shelters were distributed free to poor families. Gas masks were issued to everyone, even

blitzkrieg: Lightning war

Luftwaffe: German air force

air-raid: Bombing by air

babies, as protection against the expected use of poisoned gas. Gas had been used during World War I; it sickened and sometimes killed those exposed to it.

At the beginning of the Blitz, the British Ministry of Information told the British people how to use sandbags to shield their windows; how to put out fires with a **stirrup pump**; and how to dispose of **incendiary** bombs with a scoop and sand bucket. Shelter trenches were installed in the streets for passersby to use when they were away from home or if bomb shelters were not accessible. At night, residents were ordered to use black-out measures. That meant curtains, cardboard, and paint were used to prevent light from showing out of houses, offices, factories, or shops, which might be seen as targets by enemy bombers. People were fined if they did not comply.

It was a terrifying time for the British people, but they were known for their determination to not let the Germans discourage and defeat them. The phrase "Business as usual," was written in chalk on boarded-up shop windows, **signifying** the British determination to carry on as best they could. They were encouraged to not give in to fear or let it keep them from going on with everyday life. And carry on they did, making the best of the situation. However, the Blitz was devastating for many people in London and

stirrup pump: Portable hand-operated water pump used to extinguish or control small fires

incendiary: Device designed to cause fires

signifying: Indicating

other cities. In the eight months of attacks, close to 43,000 civilians were killed. This number accounted for nearly half of Britain's total civilian deaths for the entire war. One of every six Londoners had their home damaged or destroyed. Their **resilient** spirit was amazing through it all.

Work to Do

After an attack, naturally, there was much need for rescue workers to search for people killed or trapped beneath fallen buildings in the **rubble** created by the bombs. That was a priority. However, a charity organization for sick animals organized rescue squads of volunteers dedicated to searching for and treating wounded animals after each air raid. Thousands of animals were injured or lost or abandoned by families whose homes had been destroyed. Pets were not the only animals injured; cart horses and even milk cows that were kept to supply residents in the cities were also victims of the airstrikes. The animal charity volunteers assembled a fleet of old ambulances and created small pet hospitals to treat these

resilient: Ability to recover quickly from difficult conditions

rubble: Fragments of stone, brick, or concrete from destroyed buildings

injured animals. They also provided food for animals that had become separated from their owners.

One of the animal charity volunteers was Bill Barnet, a **superintendent** of the organization. Bill had a pet Irish wire-haired terrier called Tipperary Beauty, or Beauty for short. Bill had been working in Tipperary, Ireland, when Beauty was born on January 4, 1939. He chose her from a litter of four pups. The pups and their mother had been brought in for Barnet to inspect. His wife's first reaction when she saw the pup was, "Oh, what a beauty!"[20] That's how she got her name.

Bill was working in London during the Blitz, heading up a rescue squad for animals. Beauty began joining him when he went searching for trapped animals. She never had any training, but by nature, she had a **keen** sense of smell and soon demonstrated a real gift for sniffing out places where dogs and cats were trapped after an air raid. Some animals were just hiding, terribly scared by the loud whistling sound of falling bombs, just as some animals run to find a safe place to hide during thunderstorms. Others, though, became trapped in **collapsed** buildings or were injured in fires that the bombs ignited.

It was in 1940 when Bill was on a rescue mission that Beauty wandered off, cocked her head to listen, and began intensely digging

superintendent: Manager

keen: Extremely sensitive

collapsed: Fallen or damaged

through a pile of rubble. Bill noticed her behavior and grabbed a shovel. After a few minutes of hard digging, the two of them managed to make a hole large enough for a frightened little kitty to crawl out. The cat had been trapped under a collapsed table. This was Beauty's first rescue. From then on, it was Beauty's favorite thing to do, and she seemed to have a real talent for it.

Beauty always accompanied Bill to the air-raid shelter when the bombs started falling. After her first rescue, whenever the all-clear signal sounded, Beauty would race from the shelter and bound excitedly up the stairs to begin her search for another lost or trapped animal. Bill believed that along with rescuing people, rescuing animals was tremendously important. Beauty seemed to feel the same way. It is hard to think of helpless animals suffering, frightened, or lost, or lying trapped under rubble. And pet owners were heartbroken to think that had happened to their beloved pets. Hearing about the pet rescues encouraged everyone. Families who had lost their homes in the bombing were greatly comforted to have their pets returned. Sometimes people who had lost family members would be comforted by adopting pets whose owners had been killed. Bill and Beauty performed a very valuable service that brought healing to both people and animals.

Finding animals as quickly as possible was important, so injuries wouldn't get worse or become infected in the rubble. That's why it was so crucial to have Beauty come to the rescue. She was so much better at locating trapped animals than any human, with her instinctive drive and superior sense of smell.

Beauty was energetic and motivated to pursue her job immediately. Even when a building was **smoldering** or on fire, she would rush right in, never thinking about her safety.

Bill had a little set of leather boots made specially to fit her, to protect her paws from being burned or cut by fragments of glass or jagged pieces of metal. He knew he couldn't stop Beauty from searching if she sensed a buried animal. If Beauty knew something alive was there, she refused to give up until it was rescued. Even when human volunteers were worn out and needed to go home and rest, Beauty stubbornly kept at it. She never seemed to tire when an animal was in danger. Many times, when all the volunteers had left, Bill and his dog were still busy searching. Bill said he learned how to recognize the signs that Beauty had located an animal in distress. She would not only refuse to leave the site but would dig excitedly, pawing the ground **relentlessly**. When she sensed

smoldering: Burning slowly with smoke but no flame

relentlessly: Without stopping

something was there, even when it was under stone or brick that she knew she couldn't move, she knew Bill and his helpers could eventually get through. Her job was to make sure they kept at it till the animal was found. Bill learned that Beauty was never wrong. Every single time she acted this way an animal was rescued.

The injured cat Beauty found was the first of 63 animals she located during the war. To everyone's amazement, she even found a buried goldfish swimming around in its bowl. Beauty was considered a leader in search-and-rescue. In May 1941, the charity awarded her with its Pioneer Medal, one that only humans had received up until that time. In 1944, the deputy mayor of Hendon in London awarded Beauty a silver-mounted collar with a huge medal inscribed with the words, "For Services Rendered." She was given another award that read, "Freedom of Holland Park." This honor granted her the privilege to always have park access "to all of the trees therein."[21] Beauty was the only **canine** ever permitted to have free run of that public park for life.

The greatest honor Beauty ever received, though, was the animal charity's Dickin Medal, given to her on January 12, 1945, by an English human hero — Antarctic explorer Sir Edward Evans, who was serving as London Regional Commissioner for Civil Defense. "The … Dickin Medal was instituted in 1943 in the United Kingdom by Maria Dickin to honour [British spelling of honor] the work of animals in World War II. It is a bronze

canine: Dog

medallion bearing the words: 'For Gallantry' and 'We Also Serve' within a laurel wreath, carried on a ribbon of striped green, dark brown, and pale blue. It is awarded to animals that have displayed 'conspicuous gallantry or devotion to duty while serving or associated with any branch of the Armed Forces or Civil Defence [British spelling of defense] Units.' The award is commonly referred to as 'the animals' Victoria Cross.'"[22]

Beauty was a participant in many War Savings parades and fundraisers, along with a few other dog heroes, to raise money for the organization. Beauty lived a peaceful, happy life and was almost 12 years old when she died on October 17, 1950. She is buried at Ilford Animal Cemetery in Essex, England, northeast of London. Thirteen animal recipients of the Dickin Medal are among the 3,000 animals buried there. Her headstone reads: "In loving memory of Beauty, Pioneer Rescue Dog — Died 17 October 1950, Awarded Dickin Medal for work in the Battle

of Britain … Rescue Squad." Beauty's medals were transferred into the care of the animal charity after her death and went on display in "The Animal's War" exhibitions at the Imperial War Museum North in Stretford, England.

6

Judy, the Dog Who Became a Prisoner

World War II — 1942	From Singapore to Burma, Southeast Asia

A couple of years before the start of World War II, British **gunboats** patrolled the Yangtze River in Shanghai, enforcing British treaty rights under the treaties that China had started to sign following her defeat during the first Opium War with Britain. The First Opium War was fought from 1839 to 1842 between China and the United Kingdom, triggered by the Chinese government's campaign to enforce its prohibition against **opium** trafficking by British merchants. It was prohibited because of its highly addictive and harmful nature.

gunboats: Armed vessels with relatively small cannons or a mix of artillery and machine guns

opium: Drug prepared from the juice of the opium poppy, used as a medicine

pointer: Any breed of hunting dog that stops and aims its muzzle at the game it is hunting

A Pup

When the gunboat HMS *Gnat* was refueling in Shanghai, China, in 1936, the Royal Navy soldiers on board spied a brown and white puppy for sale and decided to buy her. They had been trying to decide what kind of animal to get for their ship's mascot. She was an active, friendly **pointer**, and they decided to name her

Judy of **Sussex**. The position of "keeper of the ship's dog" fell upon Seaman Jan "Tankey" Cooper. He was a wise choice, as he was the ship's butcher and had access to tasty bones and leftover chunks of meat. Tankey fixed up an empty ammunitions crate to make a bed for Judy, although she often curled up next to a member of the ship's crew. Belonging to no one and yet to everyone, Judy quickly became loved by all the men aboard and was getting accustomed to life on the ship.

Sussex: County in England where many of the men came from

Warning

junks: Type of Chinese sailing ships

loot: Climb aboard to steal valuables

It wasn't long before her keen sense of smell began to benefit the crew. One night she woke up at 3 a.m. and alerted the men to two approaching Yangtze River pirate **junks**. They intended to sneak up on the HMS *Gnat*, catch it with their ropes, climb aboard, and **loot** the ship. However, the men of the *Gnat* were waiting for them, thanks to Judy's timely notice. The river pirates soon realized that their prey was forewarned and turned and sailed away. The men of the *Gnat* rejoiced and realized that they owed the victory to the early warning given by their faithful, alert dog. Her actions had indeed been a lifesaver that night.

Judy just seemed to be super alert to anything that might mean danger to her crew. At another time she saved one of the men from a leopard who was **stalking** him while they were on **shore leave**.

War Comes Again

Late in the spring of 1937, the Japanese Imperial Armed Forces began **maneuvers** involving large numbers of ground troops. Tensions mounted between the Japanese and Chinese, and what started as confused, **sporadic** exchanges of fire led to full-scale fighting with casualties on both sides. Japan demanded that all Chinese troops withdraw from the area, which was Chinese territory, and when they refused, Japan launched a fierce land and air attack. So began what is known as the Second Sino-Japanese War.

China's leader retaliated against Japan's attack on August 13, 1937, and months of fierce fighting began. If Shanghai fell, it would open the entire Yangtze to the Japanese, and the Chinese knew if that happened, their capital city would be next. The desperate Chinese set up a line of warships across the Yangtze River to block the Japanese, but in doing so, cut off 13 British gunboats, including the *Gnat*. Allied gunboats were trapped.

As tensions arose between Japan and Britain, Judy **detected** an approaching Japanese plane.

stalking: Following and watching for an opportunity to pounce upon

shore leave: A time when a sailor isn't working and is spending free time on land

maneuvers: Large-scale military exercises of troops and warships

sporadic: Occurring at irregular intervals

detected: Discovered the presence of

How she sensed it was dangerous, no one knew. Some of the Allied ships were attacked. When the news reached Britain and the United States, they demanded that the Japanese stop these attacks and **recompense** the countries for losses suffered. The Japanese claimed they were mistaken attacks but paid the compensation and fighting ceased.

In early 1939, several old gunboats, including the Her Majesty's Ship *Gnat*, needed to be replaced. Judy and her shipmates were about to get a new home — the HMS *Grasshopper*. The crew had barely gotten used to the new ship when Britain declared war on Germany. The *Grasshopper* was ordered to set out for the British island of Singapore. Massive 15-inch guns protected this island, and the British believed it was **impregnable**. They would soon find out this was not so.

Faced with severe shortages of oil and other natural resources, Japan wished to claim the oil and coal reserves of the Philippines and Malaysia area, but Singapore lay right square in the way, so Japan set out to destroy it. They would also have to destroy the American naval base at Pearl Harbor in Hawaii to prevent the U.S. from coming to the aid of the Allies. So, on the morning of December 7, 1941, planes loaded with bombs began to hit sites in Singapore and also shatter the quiet peace of Pearl Harbor, destroying or damaging numerous ships, including eight battleships. Over 2,400 U.S. personnel were killed.

recompense: Pay for financial loss

impregnable: Unable to be captured or broken into

As the United States declared war and began to enter the conflict, near Singapore the *Grasshopper* was continually bombarding enemy forces and rescuing retreating troops from the jungle. Through it all, they depended on Judy's ferocious barking as their early warning system. Judy made a habit of visiting sick bay where soldiers were recovering from wounds, offering great comfort to the men. She got particularly close to Les Searle, a recovering seaman.

On February 11, 1942, the order was finally given to evacuate. Suddenly, Judy sat up straight, listening intently. She then bounded for the ship's bridge to bark out her warning. Over 100 Japanese warplanes were fast approaching. The *Grasshopper* was hit by several shells. The captain gave the order to abandon ship, and the gunboat, which had sprung a large leak, sunk lower in the water, and became stuck on the sandbar. Dozens were killed in the raid. Survivors who had managed to jump overboard started swimming for shore — towards a small uninhabited Indonesian island. Judy was nowhere to be found.

Found

The surviving crew members set up camp near the jungle, buried their dead, and treated the wounded. They desperately needed food and water. Commander Hoffman sent Petty Officer White back to the devastated *Grasshopper*, which was stuck on a sandbar, to collect anything useful he could salvage. Officer White found the ship still burning and in danger of sinking, but he also discovered many supplies: water, food packed in tins, medical supplies, clothing, bedding, pots and pans, and cutlery. Most importantly, he found Judy! She was pinned under a row of lockers that had fallen over during the bombing. Judy would certainly have drowned if the commander had not sent him back to the ship. When he moved the lockers, Judy scrambled up, shook herself off, and licked his hand as if in thanks. White hollered back to the men on shore, "Hey, I found Judy! She's alive!"[23]

The men continued searching for a supply of fresh water. They tried to get Judy to help. At first, she didn't understand what they wanted, but shortly she began pawing at the ground, whining and barking. White went over to look as Judy began to dig wildly. Water began bubbling up around them from the bottom of the hole. The men quickly began collecting as much as they could in pots and pans. Judy had saved the day again. Five days after the bombing the survivors were rescued. A plan was put in place to get the survivors home, but the journey would be **fraught** with difficulty. On February 21, Judy and 15 sailors boarded a junk bound for Sumatra.

More Trouble

The vehicles that had been promised to pick the men up weren't at Sumatra when they

fraught: Filled

finally arrived. They embarked on a terrible 175-mile hike through a thick jungle full of poisonous spiders, snakes, crocodiles, pythons, and even tigers. Judy led the march. Les Searle, her new sailor buddy, said, "She was tireless in the jungle, loping from front to back, sniffing madly, testing the soundness of the terrain, ears perked up for any crashing sounds rumbling out of the darkness."[24] Judy narrowly escaped being killed by a crocodile on the second day. It clawed her shoulder, but she was patched up and kept leading the men. Her barking saved the men from being attacked by a tiger a few days later.

It took them three weeks to reach Sawahlunto, where they boarded a train for the 55-mile journey to Padang. Joy turned to despair, however, when they realized they were too late — the evacuation had taken place more than a week ago, and the last ship had sailed on March 6. Worse yet, they found out Padang had just been captured by the Japanese. Searle recalled, "Judy seemed to sense the depression that hovered over her friends."[25] Judy and the sailors were taken as prisoners of war on March 18, 1942!

Prisoners

Judy, not entitled to food rations, had to **forage** to stay alive. She lived on rats, snakes, lizards, birds, and whatever she could find. The men were soon moved to another camp. They stashed Judy in sacks of rice to sneak her along with them. At Gloegoer the conditions were

forage: Search for her food

worse yet. Judy watched as her friends grew weaker by the day. One day in August, Judy met the best friend she was ever to have. A new prisoner named Frank Williams, a 22-year-old Royal Air Force (RAF) Airman, arrived. Feeling sorry for the skinny dog, Frank began sharing his meager portion of watery boiled rice with her. This was the beginning of a beautiful friendship. Frank taught Judy hand signals that saved her life on many occasions as she learned to hide from the guards. Judy would then go on her nighttime foraging trips and bring food back to share with Frank. She was a daily inspiration to all the men. She alerted them to venomous spiders and snakes and protected them from the guards by warning them of their presence when she could.

Moved Again

The prisoners were to be moved to Singapore, and Judy was supposed to stay at Gloegoer. Frank desperately taught Judy a new trick. When Frank snapped his fingers, Judy would climb into a sack Frank was holding and stay still until he released her. The plan worked! Judy was on the ship with her friends.

Shipwrecked

Seven hundred prisoners were crammed into every nook and cranny of the ship. Unaware the ship carried Allied **POWs**, a British torpedo struck, blowing a massive hole in the side of the ship. It began sinking very fast. The men in Frank William's section were trapped by a locked door. Frank managed to squeeze Judy out of a **porthole**, knowing she could swim. It looked as though all the men in his section would drown when suddenly another explosion ripped through the ship's **hull**, providing a way of escape for the men. Slipping into the water in the dark and gloom, Frank had no idea if land was even close by. After several hours of floating on the water, the men were picked up by a Japanese boat headed for Singapore. They were safe and bound for another prison camp, but unfortunately, there was no sign of Judy. One sailor said he had seen a dog floating around holding a broken plank in her mouth so survivors would be able to grasp onto it. That sounded like Judy all right, but Frank sadly concluded she must have drowned. He was heartbroken.

Prison Camp Again

Hungry and exhausted after three days of travel, the men finally reached their new camp and were shoved through the door by guards. Frank later recalled, "I couldn't believe my eyes. As I entered the camp, a scraggy dog hit me square between the shoulders and knocked me over! I'd never been so glad to see the old girl, and I think she felt the same."[26] Judy had managed to swim to shore after all!

POWs: Prisoners of war

porthole: Small window in a ship

hull: Watertight body of the ship

Frank and the other prisoners were forced to spend more than a year doing hard labor in the jungle, eating rotten food and drinking filthy water, suffering regular beatings from the guards. Often, they were sick. They were building what became known as the "Death Railway," as more than 100,000 prisoners and Asian slave laborers would die while laying tracks from Burma to Thailand. Frank was a survivor, but he attributed that to Judy, who gave him a reason to live. "Every day I thanked God for Judy. She saved my life in so many ways. The greatest way of all was giving me a reason to live. All I had to do was look at her, and into those weary, bloodshot eyes, and I would ask myself, 'What would happen to her if I died?' I had to keep going. Even if it meant waiting for a miracle."[27] Gerald McLeod, another prisoner, explained, "Judy followed us, a constant example of what even a dog can endure. She became a vital inspiration to us to carry on, and in the darkest days, one often heard the expression, 'While Judy can take it, so can I.' I do not exaggerate when I say that this dog, with her example of her courage to live, saved many of us who would surely have died."[28]

Freedom at Last

One morning in late August, Judy began barking and would not stop, but it was different this time. Something was happening. Frank was trying to quiet her when two men from the Royal Air Force Parachute Regiment appeared. The miracle had happened — the war was over! Frank and Judy were taken to a POW hospital, where they stayed for a month while Frank recovered from malaria. One more time, Frank, with the help of some of his buddies, had to smuggle Judy aboard the HMS *Antenor*, the ship that would take them home. Judy received many medals, including the Dickin Medal. The medal read, "For magnificent courage and endurance in Japanese prison camps, which helped to maintain morale among her fellow prisoners, and also for saving many lives through her intelligence and watchfulness."[29]

Frank was presented the White Cross of Saint Giles medal acknowledging his amazing devotion to Judy. It is the highest medal given for showing love and devotion to animals. Judy was now an official member of the Returned British POW Association in London — the only dog ever to receive this honor. She was named the official mascot of the Royal Air Force (RAF) and her own flying jacket was embroidered with the RAF crest. She appeared in Victory Day celebrations and was featured in television and news programs.

She and Frank loved visiting children's hospitals and raising money for charities. Judy lived a wonderful life with her best friend Frank until her death. Frank wrote this tribute to his special friend. "A remarkable canine ... a gallant old girl who, with a wagging tail, gave more in companionship than she ever received ... and was in her short lifetime an inspiration of courage, hope, and a will to live, to many who would have given up in their time of trial had it not been for her example and fortitude."[30]

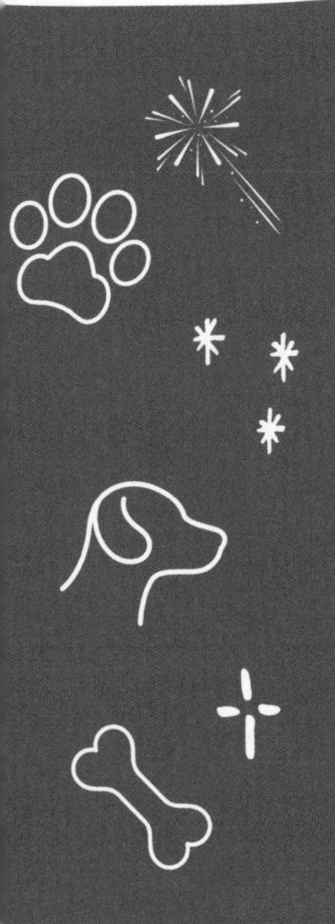

Chips, the Dog Who Disabled a Machine Gun Nest

World War II — 1943	Invasion of Sicily, Italy

In 1942, the world was deeply involved in a world war. Chips was one of the thousands of dogs used in World War ll as part of the Dogs for Defense program. He was assigned to the 3rd Infantry Division from October 1942 until he was discharged in December 1945. He served on several missions, including the Algerian, Moroccan, Tunisian, Sicilian, Rhineland, and Central European Campaigns. His bravery throughout the war quickly made him the most decorated World War II working dog.

Chips Is Donated

Chips was a Collie–German shepherd mix. He belonged to the Wren family who lived in Pleasantville, New York. His owners had two daughters and a son, John, and Chips took it on as his duty to protect them. He was energetic, strong, and very intelligent. When Mr. and Mrs. Wren heard about the new Dogs for Defense program, they made the very difficult decision to volunteer two-year-old Chips to help fight for freedom. "Dogs for Defense" was a newly developed program in which the United States military asked pet owners to donate their dogs to the war effort. The dogs were trained and usually used for guard and patrol duties. To encourage donations, "Dogs for Defense" put the dogs through a program on their return to the States to **acclimate** them to civilian life again, so they could be returned to their previous homes and owners.

acclimate: Learn to respond to a changed environment under controlled conditions

Chips arrived at the War Dog Training Center in Front Royal, Virginia — the first of its kind — on May 2, 1942, to be trained as a **sentry** dog. Dogs generally spent eight to ten weeks with their handlers learning to guard soldiers and give warning of any danger by barking or growling. There, Chips learned how to crawl under barbed wire, jump over fences, and stay calm during gunfire. He graduated from the training school in September 1942, and was given to **handler** Private John P. Rowell from Arkansas. A sentry dog was trained to provide defense around a specific area at night while accompanying its handler wherever he went during the day. Chips and John were stationed briefly at Camp Pickett, Virginia. They were part of the 30th Infantry Regiment, Third Infantry Division, whose commander was Major General George S. Patton Jr. By the end of the war, General Patton was one of the most famous military men in American history.

sentry: Guard

handler: Trainer and caregiver for a dog

amphibious: Forces landing from the sea

Casablanca: A major shipping port in North Africa

Into Service

Fresh out of training, Chips and John were bound for French Morocco in October 1942. They would join Operation Torch, an **amphibious** invasion of North Africa that came under enemy fire near **Casablanca** on November 8, 1942. This was the first time British and American forces joined together on an invasion plan. The commander was General Dwight Eisenhower of the United States. The success of this mission depended on five successful landings by the amphibious force at five different locations.

General Patton, who commanded 35,000 troops of the Western Task Force, was in charge of three of these landings at French Morocco. His mission was to capture Casablanca. Poor Chips struggled with seasickness on the trip but was better by the time of the landing. On November 8 at the break of day, Chips and his fellow canines were lowered into one of the landing crafts headed for the shore. Onshore forces of France's Nazi-cooperating Vichy regime bombarded them with heavy fire. One shell exploded so near the dogs' boat that one canine, Mena, began to whimper in fear. She was too upset to fulfill her mission. Chips, too, showed signs of being frightened, but he soon settled down and began to do as he'd been trained.

Allied aircraft protected them from above as they landed on the beach. On reaching the beach, John dug two shallow **foxholes**, one for Chips and one for himself, so they could be protected as bombs were exploding and shrapnel was being thrown through the air.

foxholes: Holes in the ground used by troops as a shelter against enemy fire

When John began to dig his hole deeper, Chips watched him, understood what he was doing, and started digging his hole deeper too. Chips and John took part in plenty of action, both while patrolling and while on guard duty. Soon, the Vichy resistance forces began to collapse. The American sentry dogs had proved themselves valuable in protecting the Allied soldiers and guarding tanks.

Casablanca Conference

When fighting **subsided** in Morocco, Chips and John were reassigned to sentry duty at the Casablanca Conference, protecting President Franklin D. Roosevelt and British Prime Minister Winston Churchill at the famous ten-day conference that began on January 14, 1943. There, the world leaders planned the next phase of the Allies' **strategy**. This is where the leaders developed the idea of **"unconditional surrender"** in dealing with the Axis powers. Every night, Chips and John, with two other dogs and their handlers, patrolled the area where the leaders met. Chips met President Roosevelt, Winston Churchill, and possibly even French General Charles de Gaulle.

John Rowell got sick shortly after arriving in Casablanca, so Sergeant William Haulk of Macomb, Illinois, took over as Chips' temporary handler during the time John had to be hospitalized. Haulk commented, "We had four war dogs in our battalion and Chips was the best-liked of them all. After our stay at Casablanca, we moved all over North Africa

subsided: Began to settle down

strategy: Plan of action

unconditional surrender: No guarantees are given to the surrendering party

and then into Tunisia. Chips missed the action in Tunisia, but after the battle for Africa was over, we trained for the invasion of Sicily."[31]

Operation Husky

On July 10, 1943, Chips became the first American dog hero of the war during the invasion of Sicily. It was a major air and sea invasion involving 150,000 troops; 3,000 ships; 4,000 aircraft; and ONE dog who would gain America's third-highest military honor. Operation Husky was the largest combined operation of World War II, when Allied forces took control of the island of Sicily from the Axis powers.

John Rowell was now back with Chips after his hospital stay. They were still assigned to the Seventh Army under the command of General Patton. Rowell and Chips went ashore at 4:20 in the early morning amid darkness and horrific winds. The landing took place at Blue Beach, on Sicily's southern shoreline. By dawn, they had gained 300 yards in from the water's edge when their platoon was **pinned down** by two Italian machine guns. The men lay flat on the ground while Chips began to bare his teeth and broke loose from John's grip, charging the machine gun nest, seemingly unaware of the horrific gunfire.

pinned down: Unable to safely perform any actions other than seeking cover

Rowell looked on but there was nothing he could do. He heard gunshots and feared Chips had been shot. John later reported, "There was an awful lot of noise and the firing stopped. Then, I saw one Italian soldier come out the door with Chips at his throat. I called him off before he could kill the man."[32] Three other enemy soldiers emerged and surrendered. W.H. Bryant, one of the other dog handlers, reported that once inside the **pillbox**, Chips had "grabbed the machine gun by the barrel and pulled it off its mount."[33] Risking his own life, Chips had single-handedly taken out the Italian machine gun nest, which saved the lives of many Allied soldiers and enabled the Allies to continue advancing on their mission. By 11:30 a.m., **Licata** was in American hands!

Chips did sustain a scalp wound and powder burns from pistol shots; however, his injuries weren't serious enough to remove him from duty, which was fortunate for the men. Later that day, his keen sense of smell alerted the Americans to ten Italian soldiers creeping quietly toward the beach hoping to **infiltrate** the camp. Thanks to Chips, they were all **apprehended**. Dogs for Defense proudly credited Chips for the capture, and overnight the shepherd became an international hero.

pillbox: Concrete guard-post equipped with holes through which defenders can fire weapons

Licata: A city on the south coast of Italy

infiltrate: Secretly gain access in order to gather information

apprehended: Taken captive

More Action

Chips remained with his battalion throughout the fighting on Sicily that ended on August 17. After that, he joined Lieutenant General Mark Clark's Fifth Army, which a month later landed in Italy as part of Operation Avalanche (codename for Allied invasion in Italy). Chips participated in the Battle of Salerno on September 9 and in the Naples-Foggia and Rome-Arno campaigns, which extended through the major part of 1944. General Dwight D. Eisenhower, Commander-in-Chief of the Allied Command, was impressed by Chips' bravery during the Sicilian landing and was excited to meet him face-to-face. However, when the general bent low to congratulate him, Chips nipped him on the hand, because he was trained to only let his handler John touch him. All was forgiven — he was just doing what he'd been trained to do.

Captain Edward Parr, Third Division Platoon commander, called for Chips to be awarded the Distinguished Service Cross for extra heroism in action. He stated, "Chips' courageous act single-handedly eliminating a dangerous machine-gun nest and causing surrender of its crew, reflects the highest credit on himself and the military service."[34]

Chips was awarded the Silver Star. The order stated: "Award of the Silver Star.... A Silver Star is awarded to the following named individuals: 'Chips,' 11'A US Army Dog, Company I, Thirteenth Infantry. For gallantry in action.... 'Chips' courageous act, single-handedly eliminating a dangerous machine gun nest and causing surrender of its crew, reflects the highest credit on himself and the military service. Entered the service from Front Royal, Virginia."[35]

Chips also was recommended for a **Purple Heart** for burns he suffered. There were objections to awarding a Purple Heart to a dog, however, so he never received that honor. Chips retired from frontline duty in December of 1943 and was reassigned to guard duty. Chips was then assigned a new handler for this assignment named W.H. Bryant Jr., who supervised the prisoners-of-war enclosure.

Bryant commended Chips to his family, the Wrens, telling them there was no question in his mind that Chips deserved the honor of the Silver Star. There was again controversy about giving such medals to a dog, but medals or not, Chips had proved himself a hero, and his story of valor was told all over the country. Private Charles Zimmerman, who served with Chips' unit in Africa, Sicily, and Italy, wrote to the Wrens, "Your Chips is a dog to be proud of and every member of the battalion that he is in is sure proud of him. I'm glad that we have Chips and dogs like him on our side instead of the enemy's."[36]

In January of 1945, Chips started nighttime duty, guarding prisoners of war in France. The prisoners were more afraid of him than the guns, his handler said. Bryant and Chips finished up their wartime duties in Austria in the summer of 1945, and finally in September

Purple Heart: Medal presented to honor service members who had been wounded or killed in the line of duty

boarded a **Liberty ship** for the States. They arrived in Boston on October 5. It was hard for Bryant to give Chips up, as he said Chips was the best friend he'd ever had.

Chips was retrained for civilian life at Front Royal, Virginia. "Mr. Chips," the name given to him on his discharge papers was honorably discharged on December 10, 1945, and sent home to the Wren family. When four-year-old Johnny saw Chips, he threw his arms around him. "I remember going to the station with my father and others and having friends around, but mostly I remember when I saw him in the cage and realized that was my dog coming home. I was quite excited, as was everybody."[37]

When he finally got home, Chips, exhausted, fell asleep, safe at home at last, surrounded by his beloved family. He was home and his job was to protect his family again. Johnny recalls the story his mother told him of how Chips saved Johnny's life. "We were at Quogue Beach one day. I wandered out to the water. Suddenly the undertow took me under, and Chips was the only one who saw it happen. He ran into the water and pulled me out by my swim trunks. He was quite an animal."[38] Chips never stopped being a hero.

Liberty ship: Type of British ship that was built on a mass-production scale to save supplies

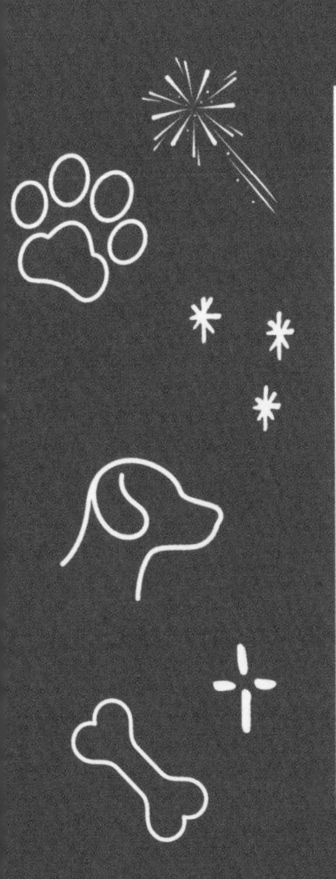

8

Smoky, the Dog Who Strung Telephone Wires

World War II — 1944	Jungle of New Guinea

The New Guinea campaign was one of the hardest fought of World War II. It was surrounded by 6,000-foot mountains and three **airdromes**. Most of what was left of Japan's air strength, which consisted of 350 warplanes, was located there, and held by their large force of supply personnel.

Bill Meets Smoky

It was in that war-torn jungle that Bill Wynne, a member of the U.S. Army Air Force 26th **Reconnaissance** Squad, found himself. His job was to get pictures and develop them, providing the army with needed information. It was here that Bill one day entered his tent to find himself looking into a fuzzy, grinning face. He recalls, "Almond eyes laughed at me above a jet-black button nose, a friendly pink tongue licked my hand. A closer examination revealed this creature to be a female dog. Her stubby tail wagged in a blur. Her size was unreal! She was no longer than my GI shoes."[39] His buddy, working on his jeep by the side of the road, had happened upon the little dog. He heard a whimpering sound as she was trying desperately to climb out of an abandoned foxhole. He lifted her into his jeep, but not being a dog lover, offered to sell her to his buddy, Bill. That was the start of a lifelong friendship between man and dog.

airdromes: Places or areas where small aircraft can land and take off

Reconnaissance: Exploratory military survey of enemy territory to find out information

Smoky Learns Quickly

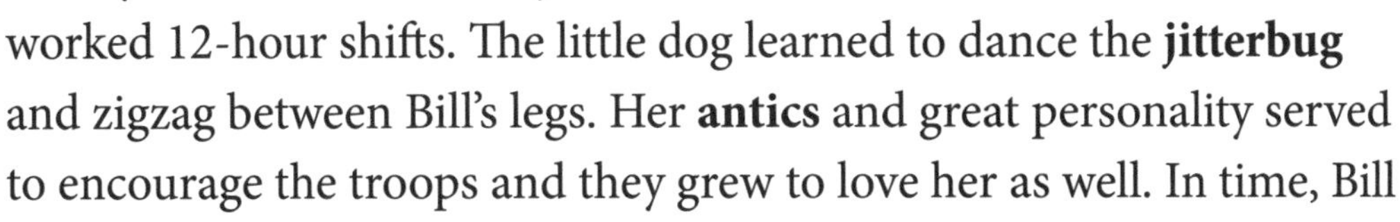

Smoky, as Bill named her, shared Bill's bacon, eggs, sausage, and ham. Each day, Bill used his helmet to bathe her to keep her free from ticks. In his spare time, he taught her simple commands and soon, many tricks. Smoky learned very quickly. Bill grew so fond of Smoky that he would do almost anything to protect her. Every day Smoky followed Bill to his job. He worked 12-hour shifts. The little dog learned to dance the **jitterbug** and zigzag between Bill's legs. Her **antics** and great personality served to encourage the troops and they grew to love her as well. In time, Bill put on a dog show and created **props** for Smoky to entertain the men. He even made a simple parachute for her. He entered her in a photo contest, too, placing her in his helmet to demonstrate how small she was.

jitterbug: Fast dance that was a type of swing dance popular in the 1940s

antics: Amusing behavior

props: Objects used in a performance

Bill Gets Sick

One day Bill woke up with a very high fever. He had to leave Smoky in the care of one of the soldiers as he was taken away in an ambulance. He was diagnosed with **dengue fever**. After three days, his buddies came to visit him and brought Smoky along. She was so excited to see Bill! Opening the mail his buddies handed

dengue fever: Type of viral infection spread by mosquitoes in tropical areas

him, he learned that Smoky had actually won first prize from the *Yank Down Under* magazine photo contest in which he had entered her! Bill was so encouraged that he began to feel better. He also learned that Smoky was a Yorkshire terrier. He had always wondered what kind of dog she was, and again, Bill puzzled about how in the world she had gotten to New Guinea. Smoky was an instant encouragement to the men in the hospital. The nurses asked Bill if they could take her on their rounds. She was a favorite with the men, making the rounds during the day, but snuggling up to her best buddy Bill at night.

When Bill had recovered sufficiently, he learned he would rejoin his squadron, now on the north coast of New Guinea. Arriving there, both Bill and Smoky shivered with cold. It was 80 degrees, but they had been in the tropics so long this felt cold to them. Bill bought a wool card table cover to make a blanket for his dog. Friendly townspeople offered him and Smoky steak and milk. Some women helped stitch a real jacket from the wool he had purchased. When finished it had beaded edges, **corporal** stripes, and a Fifth Air Force patch sewn on it. That first night Bill and Smoky shivered under a pile of six blankets trying to keep warm.

corporal: Low-ranking officer in the armed forces

Entertaining the Troops

The hospitals were **inundated** because the Allies had been in constant combat trying to get control of **strategic** air space. A nurse heard about Smoky comforting wounded men and asked Bill if he and Smoky would visit the overflowing hospitals to cheer up the men. That week Bill and Smoky visited eight wards of the 109th Field Hospital for Navy and Marines.

After two weeks of encouraging the men, Bill and Smoky rejoined their unit on **Biak Island**. Bill and his fellow soldiers who worked in the photo lab were working 12-hour shifts around the clock. When the air raid alarms sounded, Smoky was first to alert the men so they could run to the safety of caves before the bombs dropped.

Whenever Bill had spare time, he built new props for the dog show. From an orange crate, he carved a 12-inch-long scooter using pulleys he salvaged from an old plane for wheels. A soldier skilled in sheet metal welded together pipes to create a tightrope, and Smoky learned to walk the tightrope blindfolded, to the delight of the men. Bill found an old barrel and taught Smoky to walk on it across the stage he constructed.

inundated: Overflowing

strategic: Carefully planned to gain an advantage

Biak Island: An island northwest of New Guinea

A New Job

Bill was offered a dangerous new opportunity that would allow him to go home earlier than he thought. The job was flying in combat missions where enemy fire was expected. His assignment would be to look for **downed** pilots. He would fly low and slow over enemy foxholes to get pictures. He took the job and, of course, Smoky went with him. He and Smoky flew 73 hours on 13 missions in 10 weeks. On Christmas Day 1944, the troops enjoyed cranberries, turkey, and pies, an unexpected treat.

Days later they took on a top-secret mission and weren't even allowed to write letters home. They were loaded on a ship and joined the 2,100 other ships heading for **Luzon** as a part of the largest naval force ever. The voyage was interrupted by the sound of alarms, horns, and bells alerting the men to an attack of Japanese **kamikaze** pilots. Bill lay flat on the deck, covering his dog with his body. Looking up, he saw two planes headed straight for his ship. Marine gunners on deck began targeting the planes nonstop. The gunners hit their targets, and the Japanese planes erupted into balls of smoke and splashed into the ocean just in time. As Bill slowly got up, he noticed that a bullet had torn through the metal of the jeep by which he and Smoky had taken cover. If he hadn't been flat on deck, protecting his dog, the bullet would likely have hit Bill in the head. Holding the small dog's shivering body, he

downed: Shot down plane

Luzon: The largest island of the Philippines and headquarters for Japanese forces

kamikaze: A Japanese aircraft loaded with explosives, making a deliberate crash on an enemy target

couldn't help but wonder if having to care for Smoky had protected him from death. The crew began to cheer, realizing they had been saved from destruction.

On Shore at Lingayen Gulf

Arriving at their destination, the photography crew was given the order to "Hit the Beach" so they could take pictures before the main body of troops landed. Bill remembered, "I carried my barracks bag on my shoulder, my rolled-up cot on my other shoulder, and my rifle in my hands. Smoky sat on the cot."[40] Holding Smoky close to his chest, his heart beating wildly because of gunfire, Bill raced for the cover of the jungle. They had made it ashore safely. Opening a can of meat, he fed Smoky and then they rested for the remainder of the night.

The next morning, one shot signaled that it was safe to head back to the beach. Bill, the dog under his arm, hitched a ride to the town of Lingayen on Luzon, the largest of the Philippine Islands. The people of Lingayen gladly helped the soldiers set up camp. They were starving because the Japanese soldiers kept taking their food for the Japanese Army. The people appreciated the American soldiers' help to free them. They dug bomb shelters first, and every time the warning shots went off, Smoky would spin in circles. Bill would scoop her up and off to the bomb shelters they would go. Every day, the Japanese bombed the airstrip, and every day the photo-reconnaissance team worked round the clock taking, developing, and delivering pictures to General Douglas

MacArthur and his field generals. Using these photos, the generals would plan their strategy.

Tiny War Dog Hero

Wire cables and telephone wires were desperately needed and had to be placed beneath the airstrip where 40 planes were located. The officers calculated that it would take 70 men to dig up the airstrip and run the lines so badly needed for communication. The job would take the men three days, during which time they would be under heavy fire and visible to the enemy. A sergeant, noticing Smoky, had an idea. "We have a problem down at the strip," he said. "We have to get our telephone wires through an eight-inch-wide drainage pipe that runs beneath 70 feet of runway."[41] The sergeant then explained he had seen a newsreel showing how a similar problem had been solved in Alaska. A string was tied to a cat's collar, the cat was placed into the pipe, and using compressed air blowing on her, the men forced her to run to the other end. He suggested that because Smoky was so smart, perhaps she could be encouraged, not forced to run through the pipe.

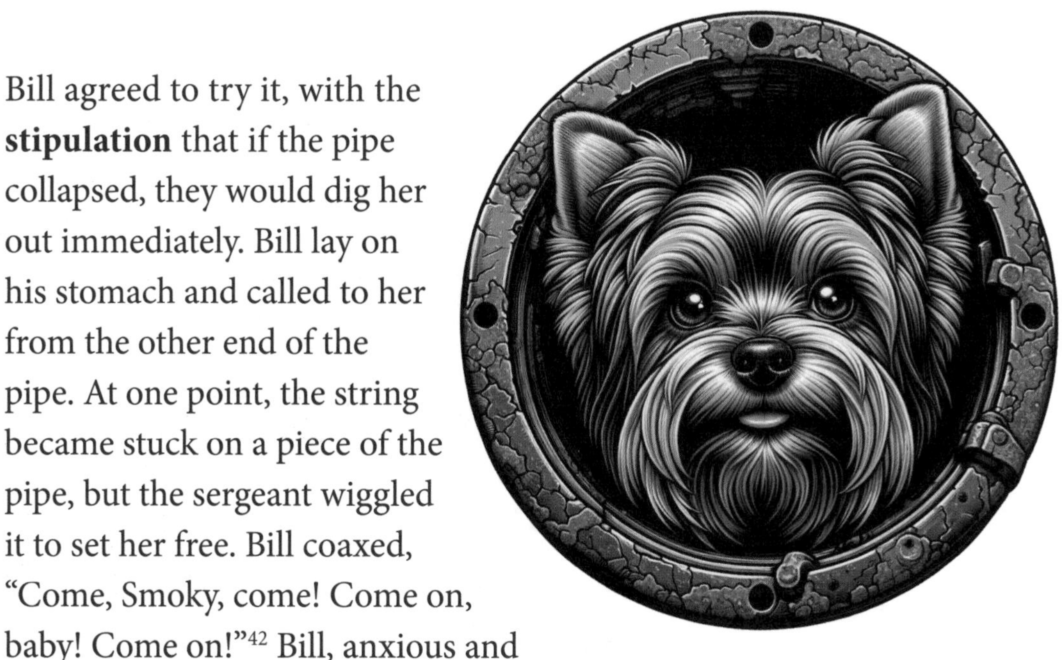

Bill agreed to try it, with the **stipulation** that if the pipe collapsed, they would dig her out immediately. Bill lay on his stomach and called to her from the other end of the pipe. At one point, the string became stuck on a piece of the pipe, but the sergeant wiggled it to set her free. Bill coaxed, "Come, Smoky, come! Come on, baby! Come on!"[42] Bill, anxious and sweating profusely, finally caught sight of two little eyes glowing in the dark. Suddenly Smoky burst into a run and into Bill's outstretched arms. He showered her with praise as she wagged her tail and licked him in the face. She had helped to save many lives that day. The sergeant rewarded her with a steak. A four-pound Yorkie had completed a job that would have taken 70 men three days, and she did it in three minutes! Phone lines were quickly set up for the combat squadron, and Smoky became famous as a war dog hero in a matter of minutes!

Christmas

One night, the men were talking, and at some point, Bill mentioned the word "Christmas." He noticed that Smoky perked right up as if she recognized the word. She barked and jumped about excitedly. "That's strange," Bill thought, sensing that somehow, she knew that word.

stipulation:
Agreement

He would eventually find out why. Bill worked on teaching Smoky new tricks to entertain the men, including teaching her to recognize the spelling of her name.

On May 8, 1945, Germany surrendered. Bill's squadron received orders to proceed to Okinawa. Smoky was allowed to go with them, as she was famous not only as a mascot but also a hero. On August 6, 1945, it was announced that a nuclear bomb had been dropped on Hiroshima, and three days later another was dropped on Nagasaki. The war was over at last. Finally, on November 1, Bill was going home. He had to hide Smoky in a carrying case he had made for her. He was not going to leave her behind after all they had gone through together. When Smoky was discovered, Bill had to sign papers saying he would be responsible for paying the large fee required to allow her into the United States. Smoky was going home!

Bill and Smoky had many opportunities to perform for audiences, and the dog's fame spread. News articles were written about the little hero dog. Newspapers around the country reprinted Smoky's story. Bill was given a job with a traveling zoo and Smoky went along every day, entertaining audiences. Bill even taught her to say prayers sitting on her haunches with her nose down and eyes closed. In ten weeks, they performed for over 100,000 people.

Bill married his fiancée, Margie. They raised a family of six kids, and Smoky was loved by all. Smoky performed shows for nursing homes, orphanages, and hospitals, including veterans' hospitals. Watching Smoky perform her tricks cheered up many a sick or lonely person. All were heartbroken when Smoky got sick in 1957 and died. An **obituary** was written about the little canine hero of World War II. Soon afterward, Bill got a call from a nurse who worked in Cleveland, Ohio. She had read Smoky's story and told him that she had lost a female Yorkshire terrier in New Guinea in 1944. Her fiancé (now husband) had bought the little dog for her from a veterinarian in Brisbane, Australia, and given it to her as a Christmas gift. She named the little dog Christmas and took the dog with her when her army hospital unit was transferred to New Guinea.

obituary: Notice of death in a newspaper

One evening after watching a show performed to entertain troops, the little dog left her side in the middle of the busy crowd. She searched everywhere, but never saw Christmas again. Finally, the excitement Smoky showed when Bill said "Christmas" in his tent that night in the Philippines made perfect sense. The nurse was tremendously relieved to know her little dog had become a national hero.

Bill felt certain of one thing: he and Smoky were meant to find one another, and he was thankful they did. The dog had helped him deal with the loneliness and fear of war. "She had lifted not only his spirits, but the morale and spirits of troops halfway around the world."[43] Smoky had not only saved lives but **enriched** the lives of countless people. If you ever go to Cleveland, Ohio, be sure to stop by the Rocky River Reservation to see the monument in her memory inscribed with the words "Smoky — Yorkie Doodle Dandy and Dog of All Wars."

enriched: Made more desirable

9

Wojtek, the Bear Who Went to War

World War II — 1944	The Battle of Monte Cassino, Italy

Poland was the first country invaded by Germany at the beginning of World War II. More than 100,000 soldiers and airmen escaped the country and joined to fight with the Allies. They were named the Polish II Army Corps and fought with the British in North Africa, as well as the city of Hamadan in Iran, which was controlled by the British at the time. Strangely enough, one of the enlisted soldiers was a Syrian brown bear named Wojtek (also spelled Voytek).

Polish Prisoners

World War II began when both Germans and Russians invaded Poland. They each claimed that half of Poland belonged to their countries now. The native Polish soldiers were thrown into prison — either the German or Russian prison, depending on which half of the country they lived in. Two friends, Peter (Piotr in Polish) and Stan (Stanislav in Polish), became separated and were sent as prisoners to work in two different Russian factories.

Following the invasion of Serbia, Russia began to mobilize the reserve army on the border of Austria-Hungary. Consequently, Germany demanded Russian demobilization. There was no response, resulting in the German declaration of war on Russia, which had up until now been their ally. The Russians let all of the Polish prisoners go free, hoping to **enlist** their help to fight the Germans. However, the Polish men didn't trust the Russians, so some managed to escape and make their way to the border.

After walking for weeks, Peter finally reached the border of Russia and Iran where he happened upon his friend Stan. Both men decided that since they couldn't yet return to Poland, which was **occupied** by the Germans, that they would join up with the British troops to try to help free their homeland. Their first assignment was to take a truckload of equipment across the desert to a large British camp in Palestine.

A Bear in a Sack

enlist: Enroll in the armed services

occupied: Placed under the authority of the hostile army

It was when they stopped for a break that it happened! A group of children who were barefoot came running up to the men trying to communicate that they were hungry. One boy came up to Peter carrying a sack. Something was moving inside of it. Assuming it was a puppy, Peter opened the sack to find a terrified bear cub looking up at him. The hungry boy indicated that its mother had been shot and through hand motions, he inquired if Peter wanted to buy the cub from him. After comforting the cub and petting him, Peter's heart went out to the little abandoned bear. He handed the boy his own army knife, a tin of canned meat, and a chocolate bar. The boy was immensely happy with the trade and ran away.

The cub whimpered hungrily. Stan offered him canned meat, but he wasn't interested. Next, he tried a biscuit, but the cub, being so young, didn't know what to do with it. Peter decided to try feeding him milk. He searched until he found an empty glass bottle and a can of condensed milk. The sweet milk aroused the interest of the little cub. Dipping a rag in the milk, Peter was able to get the cub to suck the milk-soaked rag. He was soon contentedly drinking the milk. After drinking it up, the cub turned around a couple of times and settled, comfortably curled up on Peter's lap. They drove on and soon entered the military camp in the village of Hamadan.

Peter decided to name the little bear Wojtek, which meant "Smiling Warrior" or "one who likes to fight." Upon locating their tent, Peter lined a tin bathtub with clean towels to make Wojtek a soft bed. Tired from their trip, Peter and Stan soon were fast asleep. Wojtek, however, missed his mother's soft furry coat and decided to climb into Peter's bed and snuggle up next to him. He **nuzzled** his little wet nose up to Peter's face. Peter awoke, smiled sleepily, and **stroked** the little animal.

nuzzled: Rubbed or pushed gently

stroked: Petted

Wojtek was a fast learner. As the weeks went by, he learned to eat figs and dates, and even honey and jars of **marmalade**. He learned to salute by watching the men. He learned to wrestle with the men, but never hurt them. At first, he stayed by Peter most of the time, but as time went by, he **ventured** out to do some exploring.

Wojtek Catches a Spy

One day when the men were gone working, Wojtek became very hot and headed to the shower block, where he often went to cool off. All of a sudden, he spotted a man in one of the **cubicles** who was still dressed, which was very strange and not something he had ever seen before. When the man saw Wojtek, he was frightened and began screaming. The commotion alerted the commanding officer (CO) of the camp who then held the man in **custody** and sent someone to bring Peter back from work.

Peter was afraid the bear had caused trouble, but the CO instead asked if he could borrow the bear. The man he had caught had turned out to be a spy and the CO wanted to use Wojtek to **coax** the man to talk. When the man saw the bear again, he began sweating and shaking and talking! He was indeed a spy. He had even drawn a map for the enemy, showing where things were located in the camp, and revealed that an attack on the camp had been planned. When he refused to tell when the attack should take place, Peter pinched Wojtek, which caused him to growl and bare his teeth.

marmalade: A type of jelly made from oranges or lemons

ventured: Took the risk of exploring

cubicles: Small areas for showering

custody: To hold until questioned

coax: Persuade

"Tonight," the man gasped. "At midnight."[44] Wojtek was rewarded with an afternoon of refreshing showers!

The bear learned to hunt for ants and little insects to eat, and, once in a while, a treat of grapes. He made frequent trips to visit the cook who supplied him with canned fruit or jam. He loved chasing after Peter. Wojtek seemed to make all the men forget their sadness about the war and being far away from their families and homes. He was a comfort to them all, but Peter was a comfort to Wojtek. He loved to cuddle close to Peter and suck the milk from his bottle each day.

Wojtek Becomes a Private

As the war progressed, it was necessary for the Polish men, the men of the 22nd Company, to travel hundreds of miles west to Egypt. When it came time to board a ship, Peter was **distraught** when it seemed like he would have to leave Wojtek behind. None of the men wanted to do that. A helpful senior officer decided they could enlist Wojtek into the Polish army as a **private**. This would provide him with the necessary paperwork, showing his name, rank, and **serial number** so he would be allowed to travel into battle with his troop. Peter felt a huge sense of relief — he could take Wojtek with him!

distraught: Deeply upset

private: Lowest grade of enlisted personnel

serial number: Unique number for identification purposes

The journey by ship was hard. There was a storm, and many men were seasick, as was poor Wojtek. He must have felt awful, and he moaned, perhaps for his friend Peter to come to comfort him, but Peter was too sick himself to come to the bear. Soon the storm subsided and, lo and behold, land was near. The Polish army set up camp in a place called Okonor. The soldiers once again had to sleep in tents. It was mid-February and cold and rainy. Luckily for Wojtek, he had his coat of fur, so he didn't suffer from the cold as the men did.

"The battle plan was to capture Rome, but there were high mountains in the way and rushing rivers and poor roads."[45] Mount Cassino was the highest peak, but the whole mountain range was **dominated** by the Germans. The Allies had fought for months, but the cliffs were too steep for tanks and **missiles** to be of much help. The enemies were well dug in at an old **monastery** on the **summit** of the mountain. It was not going to be an easy job. The roads were full of dangerous land mines. The men would be subject to fire from the top of the mountain, as well. The men were headed into the most dangerous battle they would face in World War II, and Private Wojtek would be there to fight or die with his friends.

dominated: Controlled

missiles: Self-propelled weapons

monastery: Type of building that had been occupied by religious monks

summit: Highest point

vulnerable: Unprotected

The Battle of Monte Cassino

The soldiers felt very **vulnerable**, surrounded by the vast mountains, knowing that the enemy could easily see them, while being

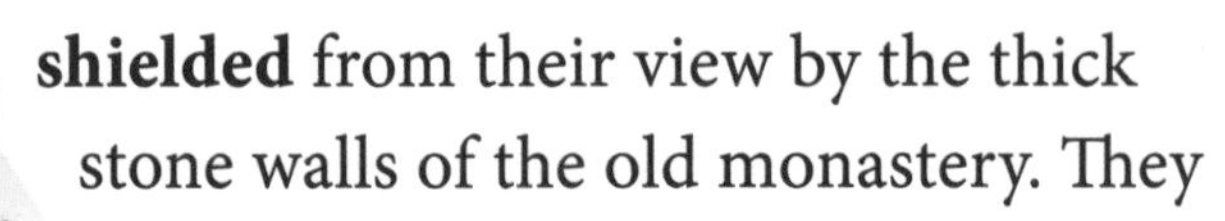

shielded from their view by the thick stone walls of the old monastery. They knew they would have to work in complete darkness and silence as they crept up the old mountain behind the enemy. They started out in trucks, but knowing that the road would become too steep, they would have to carry their gear on the backs of mules. When the cliffs became too steep for the mules, the soldiers would have to transfer the heavy loads to their own backs and climb the rest of the way in complete darkness.

Peter decided to leave Wojtek in camp, although he knew the bear would not want to be left behind. When the loyal bear heard Peter's truck start, that had always been his signal to stop whatever he might be doing and jump into the truck. He was confused. He tried to go but was held back by a long chain. They had never left him before. He howled all night. No one was there to care for him.

Peter gave instructions to Stan who was driving on the **precariously** steep road. One wrong turn and that would be the end of them. The **convoy** of trucks moved ever so slowly, bumper to bumper. They had to deliver supplies to the front lines around Mount Cassino, and then made the slow, dangerous journey back to camp to get some sleep. Wojtek acted excited to see them come back, but the next night, he howled again all night long. On

shielded: Hidden

precariously: Dangerously

convoy: Group of vehicles traveling together

the third night, Wojtek disappeared before Peter could secure him with a chain and was found waiting at the truck. Peter said, "You really do want to come, don't you?" Wojtek put his paw on Peter's shoulder and seemed to be begging not to be left behind. Peter relented, gave him a biscuit, and let him climb into the cab of the truck.

The Germans began bombing from the sky and at first Wojtek was terrified, but soon he was curious about the new smells and sounds. Ammunition was stored in heavy metal boxes. It was Stan and Peter's job to bring fresh ammo to the men on the front lines. Wojtek climbed a tree and watched the men closely as they hauled those heavy 100-pound crates of ammunition and stacked them neatly. Suddenly Wojtek climbed down and approached Peter with outstretched arms as if to say, "Here, let me carry that for you." Peter and the men helping him gladly placed the heavy box (that normally took four men to carry) in Wojtek's paws. The men stood amazed as they watched him stack the box and go back for more. He worked as hard as the soldiers, and soon became accustomed to the heavy shelling all around him. Wojtek was glad to be there with Peter and Stan, doing his part. The Allies and Wojtek were stacking ammunition in preparation for the big attack on Monte Cassino.

The attack began on May 11, 1944, at 11 p.m. General Anders, commander of the Polish Army, addressed his

men. “The hour of battle has come. The thoughts and hearts of our whole nation are with us now. Go forward with faith in God and keep in our hearts our sacred watchwords: God, honor, and the homeland.”[46]

Polish soldiers later testified that they were inspired by his words. They appeared unstoppable as they forged forward and began to pound the German positions with great intensity. Peter, Stan, and Wojtek worked tirelessly, carrying supplies up that mountain all night long. Guns boomed, the ground shook, and the smell of death was all around them, but they plowed ahead. As morning dawned, they were still transporting the much-needed ammunition to the front lines. Men were dying, and workers were helping the wounded, and the battle raged on. No one knows exactly how many shells Wojtek carried, but during the battle, the Polish Corps carried 17,000 tons of ammunition to the front-line troops and a **whopping** 1,000 tons of food. Finally, the German soldiers began to give up the fight. Bone tired, the men were able to lie down for a few hours of much-needed sleep. Wojtek snuggled close to Peter.

Finally, at dawn on May 18, the Polish flag flew from the ruined monastery the Germans had held for so long! Someone began to play the Polish national anthem on a bugle and tears of relief and joy were shed. The British flag then was raised next to the Polish flag. Wojtek was promoted to the rank of corporal for his outstanding service at Monte Cassino. The official emblem of the 22nd Company became an image of a bear carrying an artillery shell.

whopping: Large quantity

The End of War

Wojtek was with the men in May 1945, when they fought their last battle of World War II in Italy, and news came that Germany had surrendered. It was joyous news, but also unsettling to the Polish soldiers and Polish people everywhere. Their capital city of Warsaw was in ruins and Poland was now under the rule of Joseph Stalin of Russia. Their homeland was **ravaged** by the war. Peter and Stan, along with the rest of the 22nd Company, were transported to a resettlement camp in Berwickshire in Scotland to learn English so they might obtain jobs. They didn't know what had happened to their families or if they would ever see them again.

ravaged: Destroyed

Wojtek was allowed to accompany Peter to the camp and soon became well-known and loved by the local people. The bear seemed to feel at home in Scotland. He worked alongside the men carrying heavy crates of food to camp storerooms. He rolled heavy wooden barrels down to the cellar. He also kept the wood pile stacked high, carrying huge logs on his shoulders. People from the villages loved to see him and took his picture. The children were able to play with him, but only because he had only known humans since he was a cub. He was never on his own in the wild.

One day, Peter brought someone to meet Wojtek. It was Peter's son, Marek, who told Peter that Peter's wife and daughter were also alive and lived in Uganda. The women and children who had come out of Russia had been sent to the British colonies. One evening, they sat down to watch a Polish film that had been released. It was about a brown bear, and they even caught a glimpse of Peter in the film! Through a helpful group of people, Marek was able to find his dad.

Wojtek had helped reunite Peter with his family! Marek was now married and told his dad they were moving to England to take a job as an apprentice to a builder. The family would all be there by Christmas.

Peter was overjoyed that he would soon be reunited with his family. He knew God had miraculously used Wojtek to reunite them. Peter wrestled so hard with wanting to keep Wojtek but knew it was impossible. One of the men at the camp personally knew a man named Tom Gillespie, the owner of the Edinburgh Zoo, who promised to take good care of Wojtek. A plaque was placed on his roomy cage explaining how he was a real war hero. His cage had a covered den surrounded by a grassy enclosure where he could wander around. There was a pond to swim in and rocks to climb. Wojtek loved when children would visit. He especially loved it when Polish soldiers would visit, climb in his cage with him, and wrestle him as they had done so often during the war. This could never have been done with a wild bear.

Wojtek was a frequent guest on a popular television show for children. Peter and his family were now living in London, so his children and grandchildren could visit Wojtek as well. Peter told his story to many, and books were written to ensure that Wojtek's story was preserved and would live on forever: the brave and loyal hero bear of World War II. Wojtek lived for 20 more years, and "after his death statues were erected in London and Krakow in Poland, and a third was unveiled in Edinburgh to mark the 70th anniversary of the Battle of Monte Cassino — Wojtek's battle."[47]

The Korean War

In the summer of 1950, the Korean Peninsula became the stage for a dramatic conflict that would shape the course of history — the Korean War. It all started when troops from Communist-held North Korea, led by Kim Il-sung, crossed the 38th Parallel, the border that divided North and South Korea. Their invasion caught the world by surprise, prompting a swift response from the United States and other Western nations to aid the people of the Republic of South Korea.

As American forces joined the fight, their mission went beyond the defense of South Korea. There were fears that the Soviet Union and China might become entangled in the conflict, escalating it into a horrible third world war. The stakes were high, and the international community closely monitored the unfolding events on the Korean Peninsula. The fighting endured for three long years, marked by intense battles, shifting frontlines, and the sacrifice of countless lives.

The aftermath of the Korean War was both painful and hopeful. Nearly five million military and civilian deaths had occurred, leaving indelible scars on the landscape and the hearts of those who had endured the conflict. As the Americans withdrew, relief and anticipation filled the air. The signing of the Korean Armistice Agreement brought an end to the active fighting, with prisoners exchanged and South Korea regaining some of the territory that had been lost. The war's legacy, however, continued to cast a long shadow over the region, shaping the Korean Peninsula for decades to come.

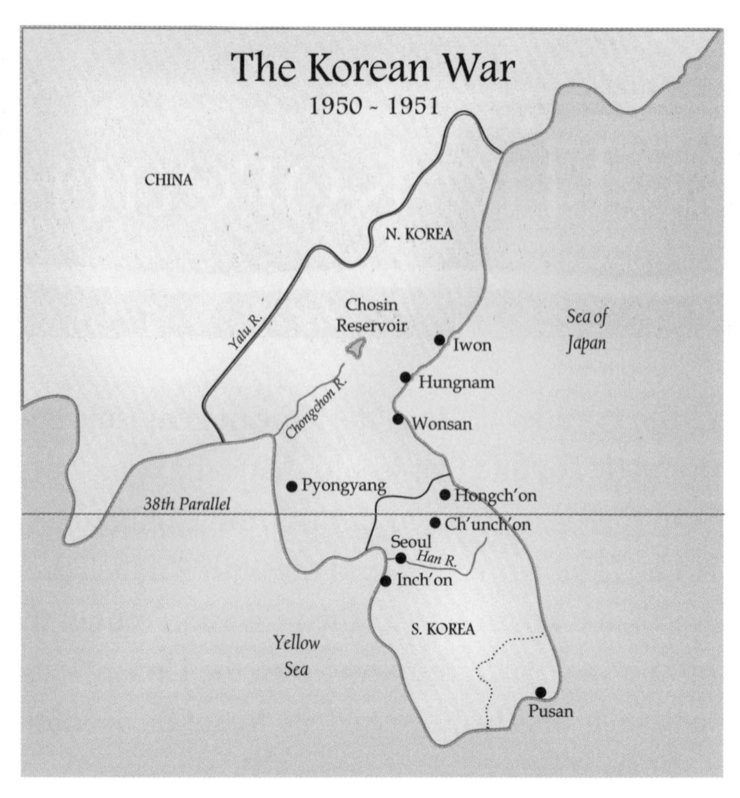

10

Sergeant Reckless, the Horse Who Carried Ammo and the Wounded

1952	The Korean War

A Horse Is Needed

Lieutenant Eric Pederson was commander of the Recoilless Rifle Platoon of the U.S. Marine Corps near Seoul, Korea. The recoilless rifle was six feet long and weighed over 100 pounds. It usually required three or four Marines to carry it across the battlefields during the Korean War. Hauling it was dangerous but necessary, because that rifle, which the soldiers nicknamed "reckless," could fire a 75 mm shell thousands of yards with great accuracy.

Lt. Pederson decided he needed a good pack horse to transport ammunition to their giant guns on the battlefield — a small, strong, intelligent animal in good shape, who hopefully wouldn't be bothered by the sound of guns firing. The horse would live with them in the camp, and when they moved to the front lines, she would go, too. He chose a **sorrel** mare with white socks and a white face who used to be a racehorse in Korea before the war. The men agreed to name her "Reckless" after the giant guns for which she'd carry ammunition. At first, Reckless devoured

sorrel: Reddish color

bread, oatmeal, or anything the soldiers ate until they were able to get her some hay.

Bonding with the Men

Reckless was free to roam around the camp when not training. She would show up at the mess hall, and the cook would give her an apple or scrambled eggs and toast. She ate breakfast with the men and even washed it down with coffee. Sometimes she'd find the cook's bunk and lick his face until he woke up and served her breakfast. On cold nights, she'd sneak into Lt. Pederson's tent by the warm stove and sleep on the floor. When the men played cards, she tried to join in; one night, she ate about 30 dollars' worth of game chips when the men weren't looking.

Training Reckless

Pete, as everyone called Eric Pederson, informed the men Reckless was only to be used as a pack horse. No one would be allowed to ride her. She was to be kept warm, fed, and well-treated. The men contributed one of their blankets for her to use at night.

It was time for Reckless to begin her training. Private First Class Monroe Coleman and Technical Sergeant Joe

Latham would take charge of her training lessons. The first skill she needed to learn was to duck incoming fire. That meant her trainer had to teach her to kneel down. He would tap her front leg, give her a sugar cube, and give her another when she would kneel. She also had to learn to retreat. When Joe gave that command, she had to learn to trot back to her bunker where she would receive another reward — an apple, a peanut butter sandwich, a can of beans, or even a chocolate candy bar, which she loved. She also had to learn to step over wire so she wouldn't get cut by barbed wire the enemy had strung. Reckless learned quickly and was willing to do whatever she was told. Pete had fitted her with a pack saddle — a padded wooden cargo frame with leather straps crossing her chest and legs. It was very **bulky** and Pete fully expected her to try to throw it off, but she just stood there. They loaded it up with ammunition shells and waited for her to **buck**, but she just headed up the hill bearing the load. Her reward that day was an ice-cold Coca-Cola®.

bulky: Large and awkward

buck: When an animal lowers its head while kicking out with the hind legs

tripod: Three-legged stand for supporting equipment

The recoilless rifles were so large they had to be set up on a **tripod** to fire. Their shells weighed 24 pounds apiece and were two and one-half feet long. A man could manage to carry two shells, balancing one on each shoulder. The shells were kept at the bottom of steep and rocky hills, so even a jeep could not manage to make it to the top. Reckless was able to carry six of them strapped to her back or up to ten if necessary. Once she was loaded up, the men would take turns walking her up and down the hill to get her used to carrying her heavy load.

The Final Test

The **ultimate** test was how Reckless would react under fire. Would the terrifying noise send her galloping away? It was time to find out. The **platoon** was ordered to fire on the enemy from a valley two and a half miles away. Jeeps could drive the ammunition part of the way, but the last 500 feet would be up to Reckless. Six shells were strapped on her back, and she began her **trek** up the steep, rocky slope. Reckless struggled up the hill and stood while the men unloaded her back. Joe and Monroe led her back down the slope for her second load, when all of a sudden the

ultimate: Final

platoon: Company of soldiers generally led by a lieutenant

trek: Travel a long, hard journey

recoilless rifle roared across the hills. Reckless leaped so high that all four legs came off the ground. Shaking with fear, she landed safely, and Monroe began talking to her in a soothing voice, gently patting her. The second blast came. Reckless reared up again, but not so high. A third blast split the air before she could even catch her breath. The horse pressed close to Monroe but kept her feet on the ground this time. When the fourth gun went off, she barely **flinched**. By the time the mission was completed, she had climbed the hill with five loads of ammo. It would have taken a soldier 15 trips to deliver the same amount. This battle was over and Reckless was exhausted. She stumbled into Joe's tent and fell asleep by the stove. He covered her with a blanket and stroked her ears as she slept. She had proved herself to be a real Marine now.

On January 31, one of the coldest nights of the winter, Reckless set out on a dangerous mission code-named "Tex." It began on a very steep hill, Hill 120, which sloped up at a 45-degree angle. It was early morning when Reckless was loaded with shells and started up the **treacherous** slope. Reckless lowered her head and charged up the hill with Monroe trying hard to keep up with her. She was unloaded and went back down to the ammo dump for another load, then charged the hill again. Each time she appeared on the top of the ridge,

flinched: Made a quick, nervous movement in response to fear

treacherous: Hazardous

the men would cheer her on. Monroe finally could not keep up with the **dauntless** horse. By the end of the day, she had climbed Hill 120 fifteen times, carrying 2,000 pounds of precious ammo to the men waiting at the top. The mission was a huge success.

Outpost Vegas

Reckless served in many more **skirmishes**, but her most dangerous mission was the Battle of Outpost Vegas. Less than a mile from the front lines stood three American outposts named after cities in Nevada: Reno, Vegas, and Carson. They were crucial firing spots as well as lookout posts that guarded each other. If one was taken by the North Koreans, it was probable that the others would be as well. Holding these outposts was key to preventing a North Korean victory.

The Chinese had begun helping the North Koreans. They were watching these outposts, waiting for a good time to attack them. It was March 26, 1953, on a balmy quiet spring day, and Reckless was enjoying fresh spring grass. That evening around 7 p.m., the quiet was shattered by shells descending on all three outposts **simultaneously**. As she had been taught, Reckless ran to her shelter. Joe gave her grain and water to last her for the night. She was wet with sweat as she had never heard such an ear-splitting noise from so much heavy, constant shelling. The soldiers fought all night. Reno was captured first, then Vegas. The Chinese Army seemed to be winning. The commanders **huddled** together to form a plan. Early on March 27, Pete and his men were

dauntless: Determined

skirmishes: Minor battles

simultaneously: At the same time

huddled: Gathered in a small space

given their new orders. They would try to destroy Carson so the Chinese couldn't take it, and then attempt to retake Vegas. The men prepared for the attack. Monroe went to get Reckless. Perhaps sensing the unrest in camp and realizing from past experience there may be another battle brewing, she refused food, which was unusual for her. Reckless was to supply three recoilless rifles at the top of the ridges. Joe and Monroe loaded Reckless' pack with eight shells weighing 192 pounds. Three shells were strapped to each of her sides and two on her back. The horse patiently stood waiting as her load was increased beyond what she was used to. When they finished loading the ammo, she began charging to the top as she had been trained.

Fierce Fighting

The path this time was extra treacherous because once she got past the first hill, she would have to cross open rice fields where she would be **exposed** to enemy fire. After the rice field, she would have to climb a second rocky steep hill. Once Reckless had been shown the new path, she left Joe and Monroe behind and trotted back down the hill for another load. Shells blasted all around the little horse, filling the air with smoke and flashing lights from the explosions. Reckless persisted on her mission. The gunners would pat her as she **crested** the hill with fresh loads. Reckless went alone through screaming shells and the continual roar of the rifles. Each time her path was a little longer, as she had to supply all the gun locations. Hour after hour she kept going, even when a piece of shrapnel cut her above her eye. Blood trickled down her white face.

A short time later another piece of shrapnel cut her side, but after she had been treated with a

exposed: Vulnerable

crested: Reached the top

bit of **iodine** and had a drink of water, she kept on going, her legs trembling and her body covered with sweat. She made two trips to every Marine station. Hours passed. At one point Joe feared that she was overworked. He pulled the little horse off to the side and unstrapped her saddle, rubbing her sides and refreshing her with water and grain. "Good girl!" he kept telling her over and over again.[48] After about a half hour she seemed revived, so he loaded her up again as the battle still raged.

A New Job

The battle had gone on for so long and many men had been injured. The Marines needed to find a way to get their wounded men down the hill to the medics who were waiting to treat them. Pete had an idea. Once Reckless was unloaded at the top of the hill, the men would place a wounded man on her back for her to carry down. The first man weighed about 200 pounds, so Reckless now had an even heavier load and no break from weight while going down the hill, but she never hesitated. "The Marines who fought with Reckless that day never forgot the sight of the mare coming down the hill, bringing her fellow soldiers to safety."[49] Time and again Reckless

iodine: Antiseptic used to treat wounds

climbed the hill, delivering the badly needed ammo to soldiers manning the guns and carrying precious lives back down the hillside. As the weary day went on, Reckless grew tired and sore. Joe gave her another rest, pouring water into his helmet to give her a badly needed drink and then a chocolate bar to give her strength. Reckless was a tremendous encouragement to the men on the hill as they observed her relentlessly keeping on. By the end of the day, the Marines had driven the enemy back a bit. The firepower was beginning to work. Night fell and fighting ceased. Joe cleaned the wounded men's blood off Reckless' back and brushed her. Trembling, she ate a bit more grain before her legs gave out, and she lay down for a well-earned night's sleep. Joe covered the little horse with her blanket.

At sunrise, Reckless was back at her job. That morning, Marine planes — during the Korean War, units of the 1st Marine Aircraft Wing flew more than 118,000 **sorties** in support of U.N. forces — came to help. They hit Vegas with 28 tons of bombs, which actually blasted away part of the mountain itself. Their plan had worked, and the enemy fell back! The Marines reclaimed Outpost Vegas on March 28 after 72 hours of battle. Reckless had made 51 trips to different gun positions and traveled more than 35 dangerous miles up and down steep terrain. She had carried more than 9,000 pounds of ammunition and brought countless wounded Marines to safety! This battle helped change the course of the war.

sorties: Attacks by plane into enemy territory

Promoted to Sergeant

The Marines were immensely proud of Reckless, their four-legged friend. They promoted her to sergeant. When the war ended, one by one the men came to say goodbye and salute the little mare who had helped win the battle, saving scores of lives and providing encouragement to keep on going. They desperately wanted to bring her home to the States. "A ship-owner agreed to pay her passage, and the men took up a collection to buy her a beautiful scarlet-and-gold blanket with sergeant's stripes. But by the time the boat arrived, Reckless had eaten her blanket, ribbons and all!"[50]

Reckless received two Purple Heart medals for her service in the Battle of Outpost Vegas. This is an honor bestowed on any soldiers wounded in battle to honor them and acknowledge their sacrifice. On November 10, 1954, after 12 days at sea, Reckless walked off the ship. She was led down the ramp by the man who had made her a soldier, Lieutenant Eric (Pete) Pederson. Cheers filled the air as crowds gathered to see the famous war horse. Pete purchased her with his own money, and Reckless had a new home at Camp Pendleton near San Diego, California. She enjoyed the sunny pastures and frequent visits of the men she'd served with. "Her story is a testament to the mysterious bond between humans and animals and proof of the Marine Corps motto: **Semper Fidelis**."[51]

Semper Fidelis:
Always faithful

Reckless made many guest appearances and joined her 5th Marines on hundred-mile marches, proudly wearing her Purple Hearts, Bronze Star, and many other medals. She gave birth to four foals and lived to the ripe old age of 20. Even 60 years after the Korean War, her bravery and loyalty are still remembered.

On July 26, 2013, a life-size bronze statue of Reckless was placed at the National Museum of the Marine Corps in Quantico, Virginia. It depicts her charging upward, with the ammo shells strapped onto her packsaddle. "Her ears pricked forward, and her muscles strained. She looks as she did years ago when she galloped up Hill 120: loyal, determined, and — above all — brave."[52]

Glossary

accelerated: Got stronger.

acclimate: Learn to respond to a changed environment under controlled conditions.

airdromes: Places or areas where small aircraft can land and take off.

air-raid: Bombing by air.

amphibious: Forces landing from the sea.

antics: Amusing behavior.

Anzacs: Soldiers in the Australian and New Zealand Army Corps.

archduke: Son of the Emperor of Austria.

Argonne Forest: Long strip of mountainous and wild woodland in northeastern France.

armistice: Agreement made by opposing sides in a war to stop fighting for a certain time.

armlet: A band a medic would wear indicating his job as medic.

apprehended: Taken captive.

artillery regiment: Soldiers who provide indirect fire in support of military maneuvers.

assassinated: Murdered.

assault: Attack in battle.

assessing: Determining.

barrage: Concentrated blast.

Biak Island: An island northwest of New Guinea.

blitzkrieg: Lightning war.

bombard: Attack with bombs, shells, or missiles.

brigade: Subdivision of an army.

buck: When an animal lowers its head while kicking out with the hind legs.

bulky: Large and awkward.

canine: Dog.

Casablanca: A major shipping port in North Africa.

casualties: Persons injured in war.

cease: Stop.

charge: Wounded man he was responsible for.

Chemin des Dames: Ladies Road.

coax: Persuade.

collapsed: Fallen or damaged.

contagious: Easily spread from one person to another.

convoy: Group of vehicles traveling together.

corporal: Low-ranking officer in the armed forces.

crested: Reached the top.

cubicles: Small areas for showering.

culminating: Ending.

custody: To hold until questioned.

dauntless: Determined.

defensive: Being prepared to attack or defend.

dengue fever: Type of viral infection spread by mosquitoes in tropical areas.

detected: Discovered the presence of.

dig in: Create a defensive position by digging foxholes or trenches.

disastrous: Causing great damage.

distraught: Deeply upset.

disinfected: Chemical removal of bacteria.

dog tags: Soldier's metal identity tags, usually worn on a chain around the neck.

dominated: Controlled.

downed: Shot down plane.

emblem: Badge.

enfilading: Bombarding.

enlist: Enroll in the armed forces.

enriched: Made more desirable.

enticing: Attempting to persuade.

evacuating: Removing from a place of danger.

exposed: Vulnerable.

fascism: A belief that nation and race are more important than anything else; often resulting in an all-powerful, oppressive government.

field artillery: Large guns used in warfare on land.

flinched: Made a quick, nervous movement in response to fear.

forage: Search for food.

formulated: Developed.

fortifications: Defensive walls built to strengthen against attack.

foxholes: Holes in the ground used by troops as a shelter against enemy fire.

fraught: Filled.

front line: Area closest to the conflict.

gangplank: Movable plank used as a ramp to board or disembark from a ship.

gully: Ravine formed by water.

gunboats: Armed vessels with relatively small cannons or a mix of artillery and machine guns.

handler: Trainer and caregiver for a dog.

haunches: Fleshy hindquarters of an animal.

Hell Spit: The most exposed part of the area held by Anzac troops.

house call: When the doctor visits the home instead of the patient going to the hospital.

huddled: Gathered in a small space.

hull: Watertight body of the ship.

hurling: Throwing.

Iditarod Trail: Longest annual sled dog race in the world.

impregnable: Unable to be captured or broken into.

impromptu: Unplanned.

incendiary: Device designed to cause fires.

Indian: Soldier from the country of India.

inducted: Formally admitted.

infiltrate: Secretly gain access in order to gather information.

instincts: Capability to automatically know how to behave or respond in certain circumstances.

Inuit: Indigenous people of Alaska.

inundated: Overflowing.

iodine: Antiseptic used to treat wounds.

Iron Cross: The highest German military decoration for bravery.

jitterbug: Fast dance that was a type of swing dance popular in the 1940s.

junks: Type of Chinese sailing ship.

kamikaze: A Japanese aircraft loaded with explosives, making a deliberate crash on an enemy target.

keen: Extremely sensitive.

land mines: Underground mines that exploded when vehicles or troops passed over them.

lead dogs: Dogs placed at the head of the team, who were skilled in following the trail and leading the other dogs in the pack.

Liberty ship: Type of British ship that was built on a mass-production scale to save supplies.

liberating: Freeing.

Licata: A city on the south coast of Italy.

limp: Helpless.

loot: Climb aboard to steal valuables.

Luftwaffe: German air force.

Luzon: The largest island of the Philippines and headquarters for Japanese forces.

maneuvers: Large-scale military exercises of troops and warships.

marmalade: A type of jelly made from oranges or lemons.

marveled: Filled with wonder.

mascot: Animal kept to strengthen the morale of soldiers.

Merchant Marines: Civilians who transport troops and supplies in wartime on ships.

mess kitchens: Areas where meals are prepared for the soldiers.

Meuse-Argonne campaign: Largest operation of the American Expeditionary Forces in World War I.

missiles: Self-propelled weapons.

monastery: Type of building that had been occupied by religious monks.

mushers: Drivers of dog sleds.

neutral: Not helpful or supportive of either side in a conflict.

nuzzled: Rubbed or pushed gently.

obituary: Notice of death in a newspaper.

occupied: Placed under the authority of the hostile army.

offensive: Attack.

opium: Drug prepared from the juice of the opium poppy, used as a medicine.

Ottoman Empire: An empire developed by Turks between the 14th and 20th centuries.

padre: Minister.

pillbox: Concrete guard-post equipped with holes through which defenders can fire weapons.

pinned down: Unable to safely perform any actions other than seeking cover.

placidly: Steadily.

platoon: Company of soldiers generally led by a lieutenant.

pointer: Any breed of hunting dog that stops and aims its muzzle at the game it is hunting.

porthole: Small window in a ship.

posthumously: After he had died.

potentially: Possibly.

POWs: Prisoners of war.

precariously: Dangerously.

private: Lowest grade of enlisted personnel.

props: Objects used in a performance.

Purple Heart: Medal presented to honor service members who had been wounded or killed in the line of duty.

quarry: Wounded victim.

rations: Alloted amounts.

ravaged: Destroyed.

ravine: Deep, narrow gorge with steep sides.

recompense: Pay for financial loss.

reconnaissance: Exploratory military survey of enemy territory to find out information.

relentlessly: Without stopping.

relay: Each member travels a certain distance and passes the medicine to the next team.

rendered: Given.

resilient: Ability to recover quickly from difficult conditions.

retreat: Withdraw.

rubble: Fragments of stone, brick, or concrete from destroyed buildings.

runners: Foot soldiers responsible for carrying messages between units during war.

salute: Make a formal hand gesture to display respect in military situations.

Second Battle of the Marne: An offensive during World War I by the British and French forces.

Sedan: A city that was a crucial supply center located approximately 80 miles northeast of Paris.

Semper Fidelis: Always faithful.

self-imposed: Job he had taken on himself.

sentries: Soldiers stationed to keep guard.

sentry: Guard.

serial number: Unique number for identification purposes.

serum: Medicine made up of antibodies.

shielded: Hidden.

shore leave: A time when a sailor isn't working and is spending free time on land.

shrapnel: Fragments of a bomb or shell.

signifying: Indicating.

simultaneously: At the same time.

sitting ducks: Easy targets.

sixpence: British money which was then worth 1/40th of their pound or 12.5 cents.

skirmishes: Minor battles.

smoldering: Burning slowly with smoke but no flame.

snipers: Riflemen who fire from concealed places.

sorrel: Reddish color.

sorties: Attacks by plane into enemy territory.

speculate: Have made an informed guess.

spellbound: Curiously watching.

spoils: Plunder.

sporadic: Occurring at irregular intervals.

stalking: Following and watching for an opportunity to pounce upon.

stealthily: Secretly and quietly.

stipulation: Agreement.

stirrup pump: Portable hand-operated water pump to extinguish or control small fires.

straddled: One leg on each side.

strategic: Carefully planned to gain an advantage.

strategy: Plan of action.

stretcher bearer: Person who carried the wounded on stretchers.

stroked: Petted.

subsided: Began to settle down.

summit: Highest point.

superintendent: Manager.

Sussex: County in England where many of the men came from.

targeted: Shot at.

theaters: Areas of important military events.

treacherous: Hazardous.

trek: Travel a long, hard journey.

trenches: Long, deep ditches used as protective defenses.

tripod: Three-legged stand for supporting equipment.

ultimate: Final.

unconditional surrender: No guarantees are given to the surrendering party.

unconscious: Passed out.

unforgiving: Extremely difficult.

unruffled: In a calm manner.

unsurpassed: Never done better.

ventured: Took the risk of exploring.

Victoria Cross: One of the highest awards for bravery a British soldier can receive.

vulnerable: Unprotected.

whopping: Large quantity.

Corresponding Curriculum

The *What a Character! Series* can be used alongside other Master Books curriculum for reading practice or to dive deeper into topics that are of special interest to students.

This book in the series features animal war heroes, whose stories would incorporate well for students in grades 6–8 accompanying history, language arts, vocabulary words and definitions, as well as geography studies and cultural insights. We have provided the list below to help match this book with related Master Books curriculum.

Chapter 1: Murphy—The Donkey Who Carried the Wounded

America's Story Vol. 3
The World's Story
World Geography and Cultures
Language Lessons for a Living Education

Chapter 2: Sergeant Stubby—The Dog Who Caught a German Spy

America's Story Vol. 3
The World's Story
World Geography and Cultures
Language Lessons for a Living Education

Chapter 3: Cher Ami—The Pigeon Who Saved the Lost Battalion

America's Story Vol. 3
The World's Story
World Geography and Cultures
Language Lessons for a Living Education

Chapter 4: Balto—The Dog Who Saved Nome

America's Story Vol. 3
The World's Story
World Geography and Cultures
Language Lessons for a Living Education

Chapter 5: Tipperary Beauty—The Dog Who Rescued Pets

America's Story Vol. 3
The World's Story
World Geography and Cultures
Language Lessons for a Living Education

Chapter 6: Judy—The Dog Who Became a Prisoner

America's Story Vol. 3
The World's Story
World Geography and Cultures
Language Lessons for a Living Education

Chapter 7: Chips—The Dog Who Disabled a Machine Gun Nest

America's Story Vol. 3
The World's Story
World Geography and Cultures
Language Lessons for a Living Education

Chapter 8: Smoky—The Dog Who Strung Telephone Wires

America's Story Vol. 3
The World's Story
World Geography and Cultures
Language Lessons for a Living Education

Chapter 9: Wojtek—The Bear Who Went to War

America's Story Vol. 3
The World's Story
World Geography and Cultures
Language Lessons for a Living Education

Chapter 10: Sergeant Reckless—The Horse Who Carried Ammo and Wounded

America's Story Vol. 3
The World's Story
World Geography and Cultures
Language Lessons for a Living Education

Endnotes

1. Sir Irving Benson, *The Man with the Donkey: John Simpson Kirkpatrick — The Good Samaritan of Gallipoli* (London: Hodder and Stoughton, 1965) 41.
2. Mark Greenwood, *The Donkey of Gallipoli: A True Story of Courage in World War I* (Cambridge, MA: Candlewick Press, 2008) 20.
3. Benson, *The Man with the Donkey*, 43.
4. Ibid., 47.
5. Ibid., 46.
6. Ibid.
7. Ann Bausum, *Stubby the War Dog: The True Story of World War I's Bravest Dog* (Washington, DC: National Geographic 2018) 29.
8. Laurie Caulkhoven, *Hero Pup of World War I* (New York: Scholastic, 2018) 60.
9. Bausum, *Stubby the War Dog*, 38.
10. Caulkhoven, *Hero Pup of World War I,* 72.
11. https://www.americanheritage.com/lost-battalion.
12. Ibid.
13. Ibid.
14. Yel Nomtov, *Cher Ami Comes Through* (North Mankato, MN: Capstone Press, 2023) 20. Also https://en.wikipedia.org/wiki/Cher_Ami.
15. LaVere Anderson, *Balto: Sled Dog of Alaska* (Champaign, IL: Garrard Publishing Co., 1976) 17.
16. Ibid., 32.
17. Ibid., 33.
18. Ibid.
19. Marilyn Boyer and Grace Tumas, *Portraits of Integrity* (Rustburg, VA: The Learning Parent, 2012) 269.
20. Robin Hutton, *War Animals: The Unsung Heroes of World War II* (Washington, DC: Regnery History, 2018) 176.
21. Ibid., 179.
22. https://en.wikipedia.org/wiki/Dickin_Medal.
23. Hutton, *War Animals: The Unsung Heroes of World War II,* 215.
24. Ibid., 217.
25. Ibid., 218.
26. David Long, *Heroes: Incredible True Stories of Courageous Animals* (London: Faber and Faber, 2014) 20.
27. Hutton, *War Animals: The Unsung Heroes of WW II*, 231.
28. Ibid., 232.
29. Ibid., 237.
30. Ibid., 243.
31. Ibid., 42.
32. Ibid., 43.
33. Ibid.
34. Ibid., 46.
35. Ibid., 47.
36. Ibid., 49.
37. Ibid., 52.
38. Ibid., 53.
39. William A. Wynne, *Yorkie Doodle Dandy*, (Denver, CO: Top Dog Enterprises, 1996) 1.
40. Nancy Roe Prim, *Smoky, the Dog that Saved My Life* (Athens, OH: Ohio University Press, 2019) 61.
41. Ibid., 64.
42. Wynne, *Yorkie Doodle Dandy*, 51.

43. Ibid., 116.
44. Bibi Duman Tak, *Soldier Bear* (Grand Rapids, MI: William B. Eerdmans Publishing Company, 2008) 46.
45. Jenny Robertson, *War Hero Bear* (Edinburgh, UK: Birlinn Limited, 2014) 92.
46. Ibid., 101.
47. David Long, *Not All Heroes are Human Heroes* (London: Faber and Faber Limited, 2014) 41.
48. Emma Carlson Berne, *Sergeant Reckless* (New York, NY: Scholastic Press, 2022) 58.
49. Ibid., 61.
50. Patricia McCormick, *Sergeant Reckless: The True Story of the Little Horse Who Became a Hero* (New York, NY: Harper-Collins, 2017) 29.
51. Ibid.
52. Berne, *Sergeant Reckless*, 87.